# Letters on an Elk Hunt by a Woman Homesteader

## ELINORE PRUITT STEWART

COSIMOCLASSICS

NEW YORK

We found Mrs. Bonham a pleasant little woman whose
husband had earned her pretty new machine by chewing tobacco.
I reckon you think that is a mighty funny method of earning anything,
but some tobacco has tags which are redeemable, and the machine
was one of the premiums. Mrs. Bonham just beamed with pride
as she rolled out her machine. "I never had a machine before,"
she explained. "I just went to the neighbors' when I had to sew.
So of course I wanted a machine awfully bad. So Frank jest
chawed and chawed, and I saved every tag till we got enough,
and last year we got the machine. Frank is chawin' out a clock
now; but that won't take him so long as the machine did."

—from *Letters on an Elk Hunt by a Woman Homesteader*

# CONTENTS

# LETTERS ON AN ELK HUNT
By a Woman Homesteader

# LETTERS
# ON AN ELK HUNT

## I

CONNIE WILLIS

BURNT FORK, WYO., July 8, 1914.

DEAR MRS. CONEY, —

Your letter of the 4th just to hand. How glad your letters make me; how glad I am to have you to tell little things to.

I intended to write you as soon as I came back from Green River, to tell you of a girl I saw there; but there was a heap to do and I kept putting it off. I have described the desert so often that I am afraid I will tire you, so I will leave that out and tell you that we arrived in town rather late. The help at the hotel were having their supper in the regular dining-room, as all the guests were out. They cheerfully left their own meal to place ours on the table.

1

# LETTERS ON AN ELK HUNT

One of them interested me especially. She was a small person; I could n't decide whether she was a child or a woman. I kept thinking her homely, and then when she spoke I forgot everything but the music of her voice, — it was so restful, so rich and mellow in tone, and she seemed so small for such a splendid voice. Somehow I kept expecting her to squeak like a mouse, but every word she spoke charmed me. Before the meal was over it came out that she was the dish-washer. All the rest of the help had finished their work for the day, but she, of course, had to wash what dishes we had been using.

The rest went their ways; and as our own tardiness had belated her, I offered to help her to carry out the dishes. It was the work of only a moment to dry them, so I did that. She was so small that she had to stand on a box in order to be comfortable while she washed the cups and plates.

"The sink and drain-board were made for real folks. I have to use this box to stand on,

or else the water runs back down my sleeves,"
she told me.

My room was upstairs; she helped me up
with the children. She said her name was
Connie Willis, that she was the only one of
her "ma's first man's" children; but ma married again after pa died and there were a lot
of the second batch. When the mother died
she left a baby only a few hours old. As Connie was older than the other children she took
charge of the household and of the tiny little
baby.

I just wish you could have seen her face
light up when she spoke of little Lennie.

"Lennie is eight years old now, and she is
just as smart as the smartest and as pretty as
a doll. All the Ford children are pretty, and
smart, too. I am the only homely child ma
had. It would do you good just to look at
any of the rest, 'specially Lennie."

It certainly did me good to listen to Connie,
—her brave patience was so inspiring. As
long as I was in town she came every day

3

when her work was finished to talk to me about Lennie. For herself she had no ambition. Her clothes were clean, but they were odds and ends that had served their day for other possessors; her shoes were not mates, and one was larger than the other. She said: "I thought it was a streak of luck when I found the cook always wore out her right shoe first and the dining-room girl the left, because, you see, I could have their old ones and that would save two dollars toward what I am saving up for. But it wasn't so very lucky after all except for the fun, because the cook wears low heels and has a much larger foot than the dining-room girl, who wears high heels. But I chopped the long heel off with the cleaver, and these shoes have saved me enough to buy Lennie a pair of patent-leather slippers to wear on the Fourth of July."

I thought that a foolish ambition, but succeeding conversations made me ashamed of the thought.

# CONNIE WILLIS

I asked her if Lennie's father could n't take care of her.

"Oh," she said, "Pa Ford is a good man. He has a good heart, but there's so many of them that it is all he can do to rustle what must be had. Why," she told me in a burst of confidence, "I've been saving up for a tombstone for ma for twelve years, but I have to help pa once in a while, and I sometimes think I never will get enough money saved. It is kind of hard on three dollars a week, and then I'm kind of extravagant at times. I have wanted a doll, a beautiful one, all my days. Last Christmas I got it — for Lennie. And then I like to carry out other folks' wishes sometimes. That is what I am fixing to do now. Ma always wanted to see me dressed up real pretty just once, but we were always too poor, and now I'm too old. But I can fix Lennie, and this Fourth of July I am going to put all the beauty on her that ma would have liked to see on me. They always celebrate that day at Manila, Utah, where pa

5

lives. I'll go out and take the things. Then if ma is where she can see, she'll see *one* of her girls dressed for once."

"But aren't you mistaken when you say you have been saving for your mother's tombstone for twelve years? She's only been dead eight."

"Why no, I'm not. You see, at first it wasn't a tombstone but a marble-top dresser. Ma had always wanted one so badly; for she always thought that housekeeping would be so much easier if she had just one pretty thing to keep house toward. If I had not been so selfish, she could have had the dresser before she died. I had fifteen dollars, — enough to buy it, — but when I came to look in the catalogue to choose one I found that for fifteen dollars more I could get a whole set. I thought how proud ma would be of a new bedstead and wash-stand, so I set in to earn that much more. But before I could get that saved up ma just got tired of living, waiting, and doing without. She never caused any trouble while she lived, and she died the same way.

"They sent for me to come home from the place where I was at work. I had just got home, and I was standing by the bed holding ma's hand, when she smiled up at me; she handed me Lennie and then turned over and sighed so contented. That was all there was to it. She was done with hard times.

"Pa Ford wanted to buy her coffin on credit, — to go in debt for it, — but I hated for ma to have to go on that way even after she was dead; so I persuaded him to use what money he had to buy the coffin, and I put in all I had, too. So the coffin she lies in is her own. We don't owe for *that*. Then I stayed at home and kept house and cared for Lennie until she was four years old. I have been washing dishes in this hotel ever since."

That is Connie's story. After she told me, I went to the landlady and suggested that we help a little with Lennie's finery; but she told me to "keep out." "I doubt if Connie would accept any help from us, and if she did, every cent we put in would take that much from her pleasure. There have not been many happy days in her life, but the Fourth of July will be one if we keep out." So I kept out.

I was delighted when Mrs. Pearson invited me to accompany her to Manila to witness the bucking contest on the Fourth. Manila is a pretty little town, situated in Lucerne Valley. All the houses in town are the homes of ranchers, whose farms may be seen from any doorstep in Manila. The valley lies between a high wall of red sandstone and the "hogback," — that is what the foothills are called. The wall of sandstone is many miles in length. The valley presents a beautiful picture as you go eastward; at this time of the year the alfalfa is so green. Each farm joins another. Each has a cabin in which the rancher lives while they irrigate and make hay. When that is finished they move into their houses in "town." Beyond the hogback

8

rise huge mountains, rugged cañons, and noisy mountain streams; great forests of pine help to make up the picture. Looking toward the east we could see where mighty Green River cuts its way through walls of granite. The road lies close up against the sandstone and cedar hills and along the canal that carries the water to all the farms in the valley. I enjoyed every moment. It was all so beautiful, — the red rock, the green fields, the warm brown sand of the road and bare places, the mighty mountains, the rugged cedars and sage-brush spicing the warm air, the blue distance and the fleecy clouds. Oh, I wish I could paint it for you! In the foreground there should be some cows being driven home by a barefooted boy with a gun on his shoulder and a limp brown rabbit in his hand. But I shall have to leave that to your imagination and move on to the Fourth.

On that day every one turns out; even from the very farthest outlying ranches they come, and every one dressed in his best. No

matter what privation is suffered all the rest of
the time, on this day every one is dressed to
kill. Every one has a little money with which
to buy gaudy boxes of candy; every girl has
a chew of gum. Among the children friend-
ship is proved by invitations to share lemons.
They cordially invite each other to "come
get a suck o' my lemon." I just *love* to watch
them. Old and young are alike; whatever
may trouble them at other times is forgotten,
and every one dances, eats candy, sucks
lemons, laughs, and makes merry on the
Fourth.

I did n't care much for their contests. I
was busy watching the faces. Soon I saw one
I knew. Connie was making her way toward
me. I wondered how I could ever have
thought her plain. Pride lighted every fea-
ture. She led by the hand the most beautiful
child I have ever seen. She is a few weeks
younger than Jerrine[1] but much smaller. She
had such an elusive beauty that I cannot de-

[1] The author's daughter, aged eight.

10

scribe it. One not acquainted with her story might have thought her dress out of taste out among the sand dunes and sage-brush in the hot sun, but I knew, and I felt the thrill of sheer blue silk, dainty patent-leather slippers, and big blue hat just loaded with pink rosebuds.

"This is my Lennie," said Connie proudly.

I saw all the Ford family before I left, — the weak-faced, discouraged-looking father and the really beautiful girls. Connie was neat in a pretty little dress, cheap but becoming, and her shoes were mates. Lennie was the center of family pride. She represented all their longings.

Before I left, Connie whispered to me that she would very soon have money enough to pay for her mother's tombstone. "Then I will have had everything I ever wanted. I guess I won't have anything else to live for then; I guess I will have to get to wanting something for Lennie."

On our way home even the mosquito bites

did n't annoy me ; I was too full of Connie's happiness. All my happiness lacked was your presence. If I had had you beside me to share the joy and beauty, I could have asked for nothing more. I kept saying, " How Mrs. Coney would enjoy this!" All I can do is to kind of hash it over for you. I hope you like hash.

     With much love to you,

                 ELINORE.

# II

## THE START

DEAR MRS. CONEY, —

At last we are off. I am powerfully glad.
I shall have to enjoy this trip for us both.
You see how greedy I am for new experiences! I have never been on a prolonged
hunt before, so I am looking forward to a
heap of fun. I hardly know what to do about
writing, but shall try to write every two days.
I want you to have as much of this trip as I
can put on paper, so we will begin at the
start.

To begin with we were all to meet at Green
River, to start the twentieth; but a professor
coming from somewhere in the East delayed
us a day, and also some of the party changed
their plans; that reduced our number but not
our enthusiasm.

13

# LETTERS ON AN ELK HUNT

A few days before we left the ranch I telephoned Mrs. Louderer and tried to persuade her to go along, but she replied, "For why should I go? Vat? Iss it to freeze? I can sleep out on some rocks here and with a stick I can beat the sage-bush, which will give me the smell you will smell of the outside. And for the game I can have a beef kill which iss better to eat as elk."

I love Mrs. Louderer dearly, but she is absolutely devoid of imagination, and her matter-of-factness is mighty trying sometimes. However, she sent me a bottle of goose-grease to ward off colds from the "kinder."

I tried Mrs. O'Shaughnessy, but she was plumb aggravating and non-committal, and it seemed when we got to Green River that I would be the only woman in the party. Besides, all the others were strangers to me except young Mr. Haynes, who was organizing the hunt. Really the prospect did n't seem so joyous.

14

# THE START

The afternoon before we were to start I went with Mr. Stewart and Mr. Haynes to meet the train. We were expecting the professor. But the only passenger who got off was a slight, gray-eyed girl. She looked about her uncertainly for a moment and then went into the depot while we returned to the hotel. Just as I started up the steps my eyes were gladdened by the sight of Mrs. O'Shaughnessy in her buckboard trotting merrily up the street. She waved her hand to us and drove up. Clyde took her team to the livery barn and she came up to my room with me.

"It's going with you I am," she began. "Ye'll need somebody to keep yez straight and to sew up the holes ye'll be shooting into each other."

After she had "tidied up a bit" we went down to supper. We were all seated at one table, and there was yet an empty place; but soon the girl we had seen get off the train came and seated herself in it.

# LETTERS ON AN ELK HUNT

"Can any of you tell me how to get to Kendall, Wyoming?" she asked.

I did n't know nor did Clyde, but Mrs. O'Shaughnessy knew, so she answered. "Kendall is in the forest reserve up north. It is two hundred miles from here and half of the distance is across desert, but they have an automobile route as far as Pinedale; you could get that far on the auto stage. After that I suppose you could get some one to take you on."

"Thank you," said the girl. "My name is Elizabeth Hull. I am alone in the world, and I am not expected at Kendall, so I am obliged to ask and to take care of myself."

Mrs. O'Shaughnessy at once mentioned her own name and introduced the rest of us. After supper Miss Hull and Mrs. O'Shaughnessy had a long talk. I was not much surprised when Mrs. O'Shaughnessy came in to tell me that she was going to take the girl along. "Because," she said, "Kendall is on our way and it 's glad I am to help a lone girl. Did you

16

notice the freckles of her? Sure her forbears hailed from Killarney."

So early next morning we were astir. We had outfitted in Green River, so the wagons were already loaded. I had rather dreaded the professor. I had pictured to myself a very dignified, bespectacled person, and I mentally stood in awe of his great learning. Imagine my surprise when a boyish, laughing young man introduced himself as Professor Glenholdt. He was so jolly, so unaffected, and so altogether likable, that my fear vanished and I enjoyed the prospect of his company. Mr. Haynes and his friend Mr. Struble on their wagon led the way, then we followed, and after us came Mrs. O'Shaughnessy, and Miss Hull brought up the rear, with the professor riding horseback beside first one wagon and then another.

So we set out. There was a great jangling and banging, for our tin camp-stoves kept the noise going. Neither the children nor I can ride under cover on a wagon, we get so sick; so there we were, perched high up on great rolls of bedding and a tent. I reckon we looked funny to the "onlookers looking on" as we clattered down the street; but we were off and that meant a heap.

All the morning our way lay up the beautiful river, past the great red cliffs and through tiny green parks, but just before noon the road wound itself up on to the mesa, which is really the beginning of the desert. We crowded into the shadow of the wagons to eat our midday meal; but we could not stop long, because it was twenty-eight miles to where we could get water for the horses when we should camp that night. So we wasted no time.

Shortly after noon we could see white clouds of alkali dust ahead. By and by we came up with the dust-raisers. The children and I had got into the buckboard with Mrs. O'Shaughnessy and Miss Hull, so as to ride easier and be able to gossip, and we had driven ahead of the wagons, so as to avoid the stinging dust.

# THE START

The sun was just scorching when we over-
took the funniest layout I have seen since
Cora Belle [1] drove up to our door the first
time. In a wobbly old buckboard sat a
young couple completely engrossed by each
other. That he was a Westerner we knew by
his cowboy hat and boots; that she was an
Easterner, by her not knowing how to dress for
the ride across the desert. She wore a foolish
little chiffon hat which the alkali dust had
ruined, and all the rest of her clothes matched.
But over them the enterprising young man
had raised one of those big old sunshades
that had lettering on them. It kept wobbling
about in the socket he had improvised; one
minute we could see "Tea"; then a rut in the
road would swing "Coffee" around. Their
sunshade kept revolving about that way, and
sometimes their heads revolved a little bit,
too. We could hear a word occasionally and
knew they were having a great deal of fun

[1] The story of Cora Belle is told in *Letters of a Woman
Homesteader*.

at our expense; but we were amused ourselves, so we did n't care. They would drive along slowly until we almost reached them; then they would whip up and raise such a dust that we were almost choked.

Mrs. O'Shaughnessy determined to drive ahead; so she trotted up alongside, but she could not get ahead. The young people were giggling. Mrs. O'Shaughnessy does n't like to be the joke all the time. Suddenly she leaned over toward them and said: "Will ye tell me something?" Oh, yes, they would. "Then," she said, "which of you are Tea and which Coffee?"

Their answer was to drive up faster and stir up a powerful lot of dust. They kept pretty well ahead after that, but at sundown we came up with them at the well where we were to camp. This well had been sunk by the county for the convenience of travelers, and we were mighty thankful to find it. It came out that our young couple were bride and groom. They had never seen each other until the night before, having met through a matrimonial paper. They had met in Green River and were married that morning, and the young husband was taking her away up to Pinedale to his ranch.

They must have been ideally happy, for they had forgotten their mess-box, and had only a light lunch. They had only their lap-robe for bedding. They were in a predicament; but the girl's chief concern was lest "Honey-bug" should let the wolves get her. Though it is scorching hot on the desert by day, the nights are keenly cool, and I was wondering how they would manage with only their lap-robe, when Mrs. O'Shaughnessy, who cannot hold malice, made a round of the camp, getting a blanket here and a coat there, until she had enough to make them comfortable. Then she invited them to take their meals with us until they could get to where they could help themselves.

I think we all enjoyed camp that night, for we were all tired. We were in a shallow little cañon, — not a tree, not even a bush except sage-brush. Luckily, there was plenty of that, so we had roaring fires. We sat around the fire talking as the blue shadows faded into gray dusk and the big stars came out. The newly-weds were, as the bride put it, "so full of happiness they had nothing to put it in." Certainly their spirits overflowed. They were eager to talk of themselves and we did n't mind listening.

They are Mr. and Mrs. Tom Burney. She is the oldest of a large family of children and has had to "work out ever since she was big enough to get a job." The people she had worked for rather frowned upon any matrimonial ventures, and as no provision was made for "help" entertaining company, she had never had a "beau." One day she got hold of a matrimonial paper and saw Mr. Burney's ad. She answered and they corresponded for several months. We were just in time to "catch it," as Mr. Haynes — who is a confirmed bachelor — disgustedly

# THE START

remarked. Personally, I am glad ; I like them much better than I thought I should when they were raising so much dust so unnecessarily.

I must close this letter, as I see the men are about ready to start. The children are standing the trip well, except that Robert is a little sun-blistered. Did I tell you we left Junior with his grandmother? Even though I have the other three, my heart is hungry for my " big boy," who is only a baby, too. He is such a precious little man. I wish you could see him !

With a heart very full of love for you,

E. R. S.

# III

## EDEN VALLEY

DEAR MRS. CONEY, —

We are almost across the desert, and I am really becoming interested. The difficulties some folks work under are enough to make many of us ashamed. In the very center of the desert is a little settlement called Eden Valley. Imagination must have had a heap to do with its name, but one thing is certain : the serpent will find the crawling rather bad if he attempts to enter *this* Eden, for the sand is hot ; the alkali and the cactus are there, so it must be a serpentless Eden. The settlers have made a long canal and bring their water many miles. They say the soil is splendid, and they don't have much stone ; but it is such a flat place ! I wonder how they get the water to run when they irrigate.

## EDEN VALLEY

We saw many deserted homes. Hope's skeletons they are, with their yawning doors and windows like eyeless sockets. Some of the houses, which looked as if they were deserted, held families. We camped near one such. Mrs. O'Shaughnessy and I went up to the house to buy some eggs. A hopeless-looking woman came to the door. The hot winds and the alkali dust had tanned her skin and bleached her hair; both were a gray-brown. Her eyes were blue, but were so tired-looking that I could hardly see for the tears.

"No," she said, "we ain't got no eggs. We ain't got no chickens. You see this ground is sandy, and last year the wind blowed awful hard and all the grain blowed out, so we did n't have no chance to raise chickens. We had no feed and no money to buy feed, so we had to kill our chickens to save their lives. We et 'em. They would have starved anyway."

Then we tried for some vegetables. "Well,"

25

she said, "they ain't much to look at; maybe
you 'll not want 'em. Our garden ain't much
this year. Pa has had to work out all the
time. The kids and me put in some seed —
all we had — with a hoe. We ain't got no
horse; our team died last winter. We did n't
have much feed and it was shore a hard winter. We hated to see old Nick and Fanny
die. They were just like ones of the family.
We drove 'em clean from Missouri, too. But
they died, and what hurt me most was, pa
'lowed it would be a turrible waste not to
skin 'em. I begged him not to. Land knows
the pore old things was entitled to their
hides, they got so little else; but pa said it
did n't make no difference to them whether
they had any hide or not, and that the skins
would sell for enough to get the kids some
shoes. And they did. A Jew junk man came
through and give pa three dollars for the two
hides, and that paid for a pair each for Johnny
and Eller.

"Pa hated as bad as we did to lose our

faithful old friends, and all the winter long we grieved, the kids and me. Every time the coyotes yelped we knew they were gathering to gnaw poor old Nick and Fan's bones. And pa, to keep from crying himself when the kids and me would be sobbin', would scold us. 'My goodness,' he would say, 'the horses are dead and they don't know nothin' about cold and hunger. They don't know nothin' about sore shoulders and hard pulls now, so why don't you shut up and let them and me rest in peace?' But that was only pa's way of hidin' the tears.

"When spring came the kids and me gathered all the bones and hair we could find of our good old team, and buried 'em where you see that green spot. That's grass. We scooped all the trash out of the mangers, and spread it over the grave, and the timothy and the red-top seed in the trash came up and growed. I'd liked to have put some flowers there, but we had no seed."

She wiped her face on her apron, and gathered an armful of cabbage; it had not headed but was the best she had. Mrs. O'Shaughnessy seemed possessed; she bought stuff she knew she would have to throw away, but she did n't offer one word of sympathy. I felt plumb out of patience with her, for usually she can say the most comforting things.

"Why don't you leave this place? Why not go away somewhere else, where it will not be so hard to start?" I asked.

"Oh, 'cause pa's heart is just set on making a go of it here, and we would be just as pore anywhere else. We have tried a heap of times to start a home, and we 've worked hard, but we were never so pore before. We have been here three years and we can prove up soon; then maybe we can go away and work somewhere, enough to get a team anyway. Pa has already worked out his water-right, — he 's got water for all his land paid for, if we only had a team to plough with. But we 'll get it. Pa's been workin' all summer in the hay, and he ought to have a little stake saved.

28

## EDEN VALLEY

Then the sheep-men will be bringin' in their herds soon 's frost comes and pa 'lows to get a job herdin'. Anyway, we got to stick. We ain't got no way to get away and all we got is right here. Every last dollar we had has went into improvin' this place. If pore old hard-worked pa can stand it, the kids and me can. We ain't seen pa for two months, not sence hayin' began, but we work all we can to shorten the days; and we sure do miss pore old Nick and Fan."

We gathered up as much of the vegetables as we could carry. Mrs. O'Shaughnessy paid, and we started homeward, promising to send for the rest of the beets and potatoes. On the way we met two children, and knew them at once for " Johnny and Eller." They had pails, and were carrying water from the stream and pouring it on the green spot that covered Nick and Fan. We promised them each a dime if they would bring the vegetables we had left. Their little faces shone, and we had to hurry all we could to get supper ready

29

before they came; for we were determined
they should eat supper with us.

We told the men before the little tykes
came. So Mr. Struble let Johnny shoot his gun
and both youngsters rode Chub and Antifat
to water. They were bright little folks and
their outlook upon life is not so flat and color-
less as their mother's is. A day holds a world
of chance for them. They were saving their
money, they told us, "to buy some house
plants for ma." Johnny had a dollar which a
sheep-man had given him for taking care of
a sore-footed dog. Ella had a dime which a
man had given her for filling his water-bag.
They both hoped to pull wool off dead sheep
and make some more money that way. They
had quite made up their minds about what
they wanted to get: it must be house plants
for ma; but still they both wished they could
get some little thing for pa. They were not
pert or forward in any way, but they answered readily and we all drew them out,
even the newly-weds.

# EDEN VALLEY

After supper the men took their guns and went out to shoot sage-hens. Johnny went with Mr. Haynes and Mr. Struble. Miss Hull walked back with Ella, and we sent Mrs. Sanders a few cans of fruit. Mrs. O'Shaughnessy and I washed the dishes. We were talking of the Sanders family. Mrs. O'Shaughnessy was disgusted with me because I wept.

"You think it is a soft heart you have, but it is only your head that is soft. Of course they are having a hard time. What of it? The very root of independence is hard times. That's the way America was founded; that is why it stands so firmly. Hard times is what makes sound characters. And them kids are getting a new hold on character that was very near run to seed in the parents. Johnny will be tax-assessor yet, I'll bet you, and you just watch that Eller. It won't surprise me a bit to see her county superintendent of schools. The parents most likely never would make anything; but having just only a pa and a ma and getting the very hard licks them kids are getting now, is what is going to make them something more than a pa and a ma."

Mrs. O'Shaughnessy is very wise, but sometimes she seems absolutely heartless.

The men did n't bring back much game; each had left a share with Mrs. Sanders.

Next morning we were astir early. We pulled out of camp just as the first level rays of the sun shot across the desolate, flat country. We crossed the flat little stream with its soft sandy banks. A willow here and there along the bank and the blue, distant mountains and some lonesome buttes were all there was to break the monotony. Yet we saw some prosperous-looking places with many haystacks. I looked back once toward the Sanders cabin. The blue smoke was just beginning to curl upward from the stove pipe. The green spot looked vividly green against the dim prospect. Poor pa and poor ma! Even if they could be *nothing* more, I wish at least that they need not have given up Nick and Fan!

# EDEN VALLEY

Mr. Haynes told us at breakfast that we would camp only one more night on the desert. I am so glad of that. The newly-weds will leave us in two more days. I'm rather sorry; they are much nicer than I thought they would be. They have invited us to stay with them on our way back. Well, I must stop. I wish I could put some of this clean morning air inside your apartments.

With much love,<br>E. R. S.

## IV

CRAZY OLAF AND OTHERS

In Camp, August 31, 1914.

DEAR MRS. CONEY, —

We are across the desert, and camped for a few days' fishing on a shady, bowery little stream. We have had two frosty nights and there are trembling golden groves on every hand. Four men joined us at Newfork, and the bachelors have gone on; but Mr. Stewart wanted to rest the "beasties" and we all wanted to fish, so we camped for a day or two.

The twenty-eighth was the warmest day we have had, the most disagreeable in every way. Not a breath of air stirred except an occasional whirlwind, which was hot and threw sand and dust over us. We could see the heat glimmering, and not a tree nor a green spot. The mountains looked no nearer.

## CRAZY OLAF AND OTHERS

I am afraid we *all* rather wished we were at home. Water was getting very scarce, so the men wanted to reach by noon a long, low valley they knew of; for sometimes water could be found in a buried river-bed there, and they hoped to find enough for the horses. But a little after noon we came to the spot, and only dry, glistening sand met our eyes. The men emptied the water-bags for the horses; they all had a little water. We had to be saving, so none of us washed our dust-grimed faces.

We were sitting in the scant shadow of the wagons eating our dinner when we were startled to see a tall, bare-headed man come racing down the draw. His clothes and shoes were in tatters; there were great blisters on his arms and shoulders where the sun had burned him; his eyes were swollen and red, and his lips were cracked and bloody. His hair was so white and so dusty that altogether he was a pitiful-looking object. He greeted us pleasantly, and said that his name was

# LETTERS ON AN ELK HUNT

Olaf Swanson and that he was a sheep-herder; that he had seen us and had come to ask for a little smoking. By that he meant tobacco.

Mrs. O'Shaughnessy was eyeing him very closely. She asked him when he had eaten. That morning, he said. She asked him *what* he had eaten; he told her cactus balls and a little rabbit. I saw her exchange glances with Professor Glenholdt, and she left her dinner to get out her war-bag.

She called Olaf aside and gently dressed his blisters with listerine; after she had helped him to clean his mouth she said to him, "Now, Olaf, sit by me and eat; show me how much you can eat. Then tell me what you mean by saying you are a sheep-herder; don't you think we know there will be no sheep on the desert before there is snow to make water for them?"

"I am what I say I am," he said. "I am not herding now because sorrow has drove me to dig wells. It is sorrow for horses.

36

## CRAZY OLAF AND OTHERS

Have you not seen their bones every mile or so along this road? Them 's markers. Every pile of bones marks where man's most faithful friend has laid down at last: most of 'em died in the harness and for want of water.

"I killed a horse once. I was trying to have a good time. I had been out with sheep for months and had n't seen any one but my pardner. We planned to have a rippin' good time when we took the sheep in off the summer range and drew our pay. You don't know how people-hungry a man gets livin' out. So my pardner and me layed out to have one spree. We had a neat little bunch of money, but when we got to town we felt lost as sheep. We did n't know nobody but the bartender. We kept taking a drink now and then just so as to have him to talk to. Finally, he told us there was going to be a dance that night, so we asked around and found we could get tickets for two dollars each. Sam said he'd like to go. We bought tickets.

"Somehow or another they knew us for

sheep-herders, and every once in a while somebody would *baa-baa* at us. We had a couple of dances, but after that we could n't get a pardner. After midnight things begun to get pretty noisy. Sam and me was settin' wonderin' if we were havin' a good time, when a fellow stepped on Sam's foot and said *baa*. I rose up and was goin' to smash him, but Sam collared me and said, 'Let's get away from here, Olaf, before trouble breaks out.' It sounded as if every man in the house and some of the women were *baa*-ing.

"We were pretty near the door when a man put his hand to his nose and *baa*-ed. I knocked him down, and before you could bat your eye everybody was fightin'. We could n't get out, so we backed into a corner; and every man my fist hit rested on the floor till somebody helped him away. A fellow hit me on the head with a chair and I did n't know how I finished or got out.

"The first thing I remember after that was feeling the greasewood thorns tearing my

38

flesh and my clothes next day. We were away out on the desert not far from North Pilot butte. Poor Sam could n't speak. I got him off poor old Pinto, and took off the saddle for a pillow for him. I hung the saddle-blanket on a greasewood so as to shade his face; then I got on my own poor horse, poor old Billy, and started to hunt help. I rode and rode. I was tryin' to find some outfit. When Billy lagged I beat him on. You see, I was thinking of Sam. After a while the horse staggered, — stepped into a badger hole, I thought. But he kept staggerin'. I fell off on one side just as he pitched forward. He tried and tried to get up. I stayed till he died; then I kept walking. I don't know what became of Sam; I don't know what became of me; but I do know I am going to dig wells all over this desert until every thirsty horse can have water."

All the time he had been eating just pickles; when he finished his story he ate faster. By now we all knew he was demented. The men tried to coax him to go on with us so that they could turn him over to the authorities, but he said he must be digging. At last it was decided to send some one back for him. Mr. Struble was unwilling to leave him, but the man would not be persuaded. Suddenly he gathered up his "smoking" and some food and ran back up the draw. We had to go on, of course.

All that afternoon our road lay along the buried river. I don't mean dry river. Sand had blown into the river until the water was buried. Water was only a few feet down, and the banks were clearly defined. Sometimes we came to a small, dirty puddle, but it was so alkaline that nothing could drink it. The story we had heard had saddened us all, and we were sorry for our horses. Poor little Elizabeth Hull wept. She said the West was so big and bare, and she was so alone and so sad, she just *had* to cry.

About sundown we came to a ranch and were made welcome by one Timothy Hobbs, owner of the place. The dwelling and the stables were a collection of low brown houses, made of logs and daubed with mud. Fields of shocked grain made a very prosperous-looking background. A belled cow led a bunch of sleek cattle home over the sand dunes. A well in the yard afforded plenty of clear, cold water, which was raised by a windmill. The cattle came and drank at the trough, the bell making a pleasant sound in the twilight.

The men told Mr. Hobbs about the man we saw. "Oh, yes," he said, "that is Crazy Olaf. He has been that way for twenty years. Spends his time digging wells, but he never gets any water, and the sand caves in almost as fast as he can get it out." Then he launched upon a recital of how he got sweet water by piping past the alkali strata. I kept hoping he would tell how Olaf was kept and who was responsible for him, but he never told.

He invited us to prepare our supper in his kitchen, and as it was late and wood was scarce, we were glad to accept. He bustled about helping us, adding such dainties as fresh milk, butter, and eggs to our menu. He is a rather stout little man, with merry gray eyes and brown hair beginning to gray. He wore a red shirt and blue overalls, and he wiped his butcher's knife impartially on the legs of his overalls or his towel, — just whichever was handiest as he hurried about cutting our bacon and opening cans for us.

Mrs. O'Shaughnessy and he got on famously. After supper, while she and Elizabeth washed the dishes, she asked him why he did n't get married and have some one to look after him and his cabin.

"I don't have time," he answered. "I came West eighteen years ago to make a start and a home for Jennie and me, but I can't find time to go back and get her. In the summer I have to hustle to make the hay and grain, and I have to stay and feed the stock all the rest of the time."

"You write her once in a while, don't you?" asked Mrs. O'Shaughnessy.

CRAZY OLAF AND OTHERS

"Yes," he said, "I wrote her two years ago
come April; then I was so busy I did n't go
to town till I went for my year's supplies. I
went to the post office, and sure enough there
was a letter for me, — been waitin' for me for
six months. You see the postmaster knows
me and never would send a letter back. I set
down there right in the office and answered
it. I told her how it was, told her I was coming after her soon as I could find time. You
see, she refuses to come to me 'cause I am so
far from the railroad, and she is afraid of Indians and wild animals."

"Have you got your answer?" asked
Elizabeth.

"No," he said, "I ain't had time yet to go,
but I kind of wish somebody would think to
bring the mail. Not many people pass here,
only when the open season takes hunters to
the mountains. When you people come back
will you stop and ask for the mail for me?"

We promised.

In the purple and amber light of a new day

43

we were about, and soon were on the road.
By nightfall we had bidden the desert a glad
farewell, and had camped on a large stream
among trees. How glad we were to see so
much water and such big cottonwoods! Mr.
and Mrs. Burney were within a day's drive of
home, so they left us. This camp is at Newfork, and our party has four new members: a
doctor, a moving-picture man, and two geo-
logical fellows. They have gone on, but we
will join them soon.

Just across the creek from us is the cabin
of a new settler. Mrs. O'Shaughnessy and I
slept together last night, — only we could n't
sleep for the continual, whining cry of a sick
baby at the cabin. So after a while we rose
and dressed and crossed over to see if we
could be of any help. We found a woefully
distressed young couple. Their first child,
about a year old, was very sick. They did n't
know what to do for it; and she was afraid to
stay alone while he went for help.

They were powerfully glad to see us, and

44

the young father left at once to get Grandma Mortimer, a neighborhood godsend such as most Western communities have one of. We busied ourselves relieving the young mother as much as we could. She would n't leave the baby and lie down. The child is teething and had convulsions. We put it into a hot bath and held the convulsions in check until Mrs. Mortimer came. She bustled in and took hold in a way to insure confidence. She had not been there long before she had both parents in bed, "saving themselves for to-morrow," and was gently rubbing the hot little body of the baby. She kept giving it warm tea she had made of herbs, until soon the threatening jerks were over, the peevish whining ceased, and the child slept peacefully on Grandma's lap. I watched her, fascinated. There was never a bit of faltering, no indecision; everything she did seemed exactly what she ought to do.

"How did you learn it all?" I asked her. "How can you know just what to do, and then have the courage to do it? I should be afraid of doing the wrong thing."

"Why," she said, "that is easy. Just do the very best you can and trust God for the rest. After all, it is God who saves the baby, not us and not our efforts; but we can help. He lets us do that. Lots of times the good we do goes beyond any medicine. Never be afraid to *help* your best. I have been doing that for forty years and I am going to keep it up till I die."

Then she told us story after story — told us how her different ambitions had "boosted" her along, had made her swim when she just wanted to float. "I was married when I was sixteen, and of course, my first ambition was to own a home for Dave. My man was poor. He had a horse, and his folks gave him another. My father gave me a heifer, and mother fitted me out with a bed. That was counted a pretty good start then, but we would have married even if we had n't had one thing. Being young we were over-hopeful. We both

46

took to work like a duck to water. Some years it looked as if we were going to see every dream come true. Another time and we would be poorer than at first. One year the hail destroyed everything; another time the flood carried away all we had.

"When little Dave was eleven years old, he had learned to plough. Every one of us was working to our limit that year. I ploughed and hoed, both, and big Dave really hardly took time to sleep. You see, his idea was that we must do better by our children than we had been done by, and Fanny, our eldest, was thirteen. Big Dave thought all girls married at sixteen because his mother did, and so did I; so that spring he said, 'In just three years Fanny will be leaving us and we *must* do right by her. I wanted powerfully bad that *you* should have a blue silk wedding dress, mother, but of course it could n't be had, and you looked as pretty as a rose in your pink lawn. But I 've always wanted you to have a blue silk. As you can't have it, let us get it

for Fanny ; and of course we must have everything else according.' And so we worked
mighty hard.

"Little Dave begged to be allowed to
plough. Every other boy in the neighborhood
did, — some of them younger than he, — but
somehow I did n't want him to. One of our
neighbors had been sick a lot that year and
his crops were about ruined. It was laying-by
time and we had finished laying by our crops
— all but about half a day's ploughing in the
corn. That morning at breakfast, big Dave
said he would take the horses and go over to
Henry Boles's and plough that day to help
out, — said he could finish ours any time,
and it did n't matter much if it did n't get
ploughed. He told the children to lay off that
day and go fishing and berrying. So he went
to harness his team, and little Dave went to
help him. Fanny and I went to milk, and all
the time I could hear little Dave begging his
father to let him finish the ploughing. His
father said he could if I said so.

48

## CRAZY OLAF AND OTHERS

" I will never forget his eager little face as he began on me. He had a heap of freckles; I remember noticing them that morning; he was barefooted, and I remember that one toe was skinned. Big Dave was lighting his pipe, and till to-day I remember how he looked as he held the match to his pipe, drew a puff of smoke, and said, 'Say yes, mother.' So I said yes, and little Dave ran to open the gate for his father.

" As big Dave rode through the gate, our boy caught him by the leg and said, ' I just *love* you, daddy.' Big Dave bent down and kissed him, and said, 'You 're a *man*, son.' How proud that made the little fellow! Parents should praise their children more; the little things work hard for a few words of praise, and many of them never get their pay.

"Well, the little fellow would have no help to harness his mule; so Fanny and I went to the house, and Fanny said, 'We ought to cook an extra good dinner to celebrate Davie's first ploughing. I 'll go down in the pasture and gather some blackberries if you will make a cobbler.'

"She was gone all morning. About ten o'clock, I took a pail of fresh water down to the field. I knew Davie would be thirsty, and I was uneasy about him, but he was all right. He pushed his ragged old hat back and wiped the sweat from his brow just as his father would have done. I petted him a little, but he was so mannish he did n't want me to pet him any more. After he drank, he took up his lines again, and said, 'Just watch me, mother; see how I can plough.' I told him that we were going to have chicken and dumplings for dinner, and that he must sit in his father's place and help us to berry-cobbler. As he had only a few more rows to plough, I went back, telling myself how foolish I had been to be afraid.

"Twelve o'clock came, but not Davie. I sent Fanny to the spring for the buttermilk and waited a while, thinking little Dave had not finished as soon as he had expected. I went to the field. Little Dave lay on his face in the furrow. I gathered him up in my arms; he was yet alive; he put one weak little arm around my neck, and said, 'Oh, mammy, I'm hurt. The mule kicked me in the stomach.'

"I don't know how I got to the house with him; I stumbled over clods and weeds, through the hot sunshine. I sank down on the porch in the shade, with the precious little form clasped tightly to me. He smiled, and tried to speak, but the blood gurgled up into his throat and my little boy was gone.

"I would have died of grief if I had n't had to work so hard. Big Dave got too warm at work that day, and when Fanny went for him and told him about little Dave, he ran all the way home; he was crazy with grief and forgot the horses. The trouble and the heat and the overwork brought on a fever. I had no time for tears for three months, and by that time my heart was hardened against my Maker. I got deeper in the rut of work, but I had given up my ambition for a home of my own; all I wanted to do was to work so hard that I could not think of the little grave on which the leaves were falling. I wanted, too, to save enough money to mark the precious spot, and then I wanted to leave. But first one thing and then another took every dollar we made for three years.

"One morning big Dave looked so worn out and pale that I said, 'I am going to get out of here; I am not going to stay here and bury *you*, Dave. Sunrise to-morrow will see us on the road West. We have worked for eighteen years as hard as we knew how, and have given up my boy besides; and now we can't even afford to mark his grave decently. It is time we left.'

"Big Dave went back to bed, and I went out and sold what we had. It was so little that it did n't take long to sell it. That was years ago. We came West. The country was really wild then; there was a great deal of lawlessness. We did n't get settled down for several years; we hired to a man who had a contract to put up hay for the government, and we worked for him for a long time.

"Indians were thick as fleas on a dog then; some were camped near us once, and among them was a Mexican woman who could jabber a little English. Once, when I was feeling particularly resentful and sorrowful, I told her about my little Dave; and it was her jabbered words that showed me the way to peace. I wept for hours, but peace had come and has stayed. Ambition came again, but a different kind: I wanted the same peace to come to all hearts that came so late to mine, and I wanted to help bring it. I took the only course I knew. I have gone to others' help every time there has been a chance. After Fanny married and Dave died, I had an ambition to save up four hundred dollars with which to buy an entrance into an old ladies' home. Just before I got the full amount saved up, I found that young

# LETTERS ON AN ELK HUNT

Eddie Carwell wanted to enter the ministry and needed help to go to college. I had just enough; so I gave it to him. Another time I had almost enough, when Charlie Rucker got into trouble over some mortgage business; so I used what I had that time to help him. Now I've given up the old ladies' home idea and am saving up for the blue silk dress Dave would have liked me to have. I guess I'll die some day and I want it to be buried in. I like to think I'm going to my two Daves then; and it won't be hard, — especially if I have the blue silk on."

Just then a sleepy little bird twittered outside, and the baby stirred a little. The first faint light of dawn was just creeping up the valley. I rose and said I must get back to camp. Mrs. O'Shaughnessy and I had both wept with Mrs. Mortimer over little Dave. We have all given up our first-born little man-child; so we felt near each other. We told Mrs. Mortimer that we had passed under the rod also. I kissed her toilworn old hands, and

# CRAZY OLAF AND OTHERS

Mrs. O'Shaughnessy dropped a kiss on her old gray head as we passed out into the rose-and-gold morning. We felt that we were leaving a sanctified presence, and we are both of us better and humbler women because we met a woman who has buried her sorrow beneath faith and endeavor.

This does n't seem much like a letter, does it? When I started on this trip, I resolved that you should have just as much of the trip as I could give you. I did n't know we would be so long getting to the hunting-ground, and I felt you would *like* to know of the people we meet. Perhaps my next letter will not be so tame. The hunting season opens to-morrow, but we are several days' travel from the elk yet.

Elizabeth behaves queerly. She does n't want to go on, stay here, or go back. I am perfectly mystified. So far she has not told us a thing, and we don't know to whom she is going or anything about it. She is a likable little lady, and I sincerely hope she knows what she is doing. It is bedtime and I must stop writing. We go on to-morrow.

With affectionate regards,

ELINORE RUPERT STEWART.

## V

### DANYUL AND HIS MOTHER

IN CAMP ON THE GROS VENTRE,
September 6, 1914.

MY DEAR FRIEND, —

I have neglected you for almost a week, but when you read this letter and learn why, I feel sure you will forgive me.

To begin with, we bade Mrs. Mortimer good-bye, and started out to find better fishing than the pretty little stream we were on afforded us. Our way lay up Green River and we were getting nearer our final campground all the time, but we were in no hurry to begin hunting, so we were just loitering along. There were a great many little lakes along the valley, and thousands of duck. Mr. Stewart was driving, but as he wanted to shoot ducks, I took the lines and drove along. There is so much that is beautiful, and I was trying so hard to see it all, that I took the wrong road; but none of us noticed it at first, and then we did n't think it worth while to turn back.

The road we were on had lain along the foothills, but when I first thought I had missed the right road we were coming down into a grassy valley. Mr. Stewart came across a marshy stretch of meadow and climbed up on the wagon. The ground was more level, and on every side were marshes and pools; the willows grew higher here so that we could n't see far ahead. Mrs. O'Shaughnessy was behind, and she called out, "Say, I believe we are off the road." Elizabeth said she had noticed a road winding off on our right; so we agreed that I must have taken the wrong one, but as we could n't turn in the willows, we had to go on. Soon we reached higher, drier ground and passed through a yellow grove of quaking asp.

A man came along with an axe on his shoulder, and Mr. Stewart asked him about the road. "Yes," he said, "you are off the main road, but on a better. You'll cross the same stream you were going to camp on, right at my ranch. It is just a little way across here and it's almost sundown, so I will show you the way."

He strode along ahead. We drove through an avenue of great dark pines and across a log bridge that spanned a noisy, brawling stream. The man opened a set of bars and we drove into a big clean corral. Comfortable sheds and stables lined one side, and big stacks of hay were conveniently placed. He began to help unharness the teams, saying that they might just as well run in his meadow, as he was through haying; then the horses would be safe while we fished. He insisted on our stopping in his cabin, which we found to be a comfortable two-room affair with a veranda the whole length. The *biggest* pines overshadowed the house; just behind it was a garden, in which some late vegetables were still growing. The air was rather frosty and some worried hens

59

were trying hard to cover some chirping half-feathered chicks.

It was such a homey place that we felt welcome and perfectly comfortable at once. The inside of the house will not be hard to describe. It was clean as could be, but with a typical bachelor's cleanliness: there was no dirt, but a great deal of disorder. Across the head of the iron bed was hung a miscellany of socks, neckties, and suspenders. A discouraging assortment of boots, shoes, and leggings protruded from beneath the bed. Some calendars ornamented the wall, and upon a table stood a smoky lamp and some tobacco and a smelly pipe. On a rack over the door lay a rifle.

Pretty soon our host came bustling in and exclaimed, "The kitchen is more pleasant than this room and there's a fire there, too." Then, catching sight of his lamp, he picked it up hurriedly and said, "Jest as shore as I leave anything undone, that shore somebody comes and sees how slouchy I am. Come on into the kitchen where you can warm, and I'll clean this lamp. One of the cows was sick this morning; I hurried over things so as to doctor her, and I forgot the lamp. I smoke and the lamp smokes to keep me company."

The kitchen would have delighted the heart of any one. Two great windows, one in the east and one in the south, gave plenty of sunlight. A shining new range and a fine assortment of vessels — which were not all yet in their place — were in one corner. There was a slow ticking clock up on a high shelf; near the door stood a home-made washstand with a tin basin, and above it hung a long narrow mirror. On the back of the door was a towel-rack. The floor was made of white pine and was spotlessly clean. In the center of the room stood the table, with a cover of red oilcloth. Some chairs were placed about the table, but our host quickly hauled them out for us. He opened his store-room and told us to "dish in dirty-face," and help ourselves to anything we wanted, because we were to be his "somebody come" for that night; then he hurried out to help with the teams again. He was so friendly and so likeable that we did n't feel a bit backward about "dishin' in," and it was not long before we had a smoking supper on the table.

While we were at supper he said, "I wonder, now, if any of you women can make aprons and bonnets. I don't mean them dinky little things like they make now, but rale wearin' things like they used to make."

I was afraid of another advertisement romance and did n't reply, but Mrs. O'Shaughnessy said, "Indade we can, none better."

Then he answered, "I want a blue chambray bonnet and a bunch of aprons made for my mother. She is on the way here from Pennsylvania. I ain't seen her for fifteen years. I left home longer 'n that ago, but I remember everything,—just how everything looked,—and I 'd like to have things inside the house as nearly like home as I can, anyway."

## DANYUL AND HIS MOTHER

I did n't know how long we could stop there, so I still made no promises, but Mrs. O'Shaughnessy could easily answer every question for a dozen women.

" Have you the cloth ? " she asked.

Yes, he said ; he had had it for a long time, but he had not had it sewn because he had not been sure mother *could* come.

"·What 's your name ? " asked Mrs. O'-Shaughnessy.

He hesitated a moment, then said, " Daniel Holt."

I wondered why he hesitated, but forgot all about it when Clyde said we would stop there for a few days, if we wanted to help Mr. Holt. Mrs. O'Shaughnessy's mind was already made up. Elizabeth said she would be glad to help, and I was not long in deciding when Daniel said, " I 'll take it as a rale friendly favor if you women could help, because mother ain't had what could rightly be called a home since I left home. She 's crippled, too, and I want to do all I can. I know she 'd just like to have some aprons and a sunbonnet."

His eyes had such a pathetic, appealing look that I was ashamed, and we at once began planning our work. Daniel helped with the dishes and as soon as they were done brought out his cloth. He had a heap of it, — a bolt of checked gingham, enough blue chambray for half a dozen bonnets, and a great many remnants which he said he had bought from peddlers from time to time. Mrs. O'-Shaughnessy selected what she said we would begin on, and dampened it so as to shrink it by morning. We then spread our beds and made ready for an early start next day.

Next morning we ate breakfast by the light of the lamp that smoked for the sake of companionship, and then started to cut out our work. Daniel and Mr. Stewart went fishing, and we packed their lunch so as to have them out of the way all day. I undertook the making of the bonnet, because I knew how, and because I can remember the kind my mother wore ; I reckoned Daniel's mother would have worn about the same style. Mrs. O'Shaughnessy and Elizabeth can both cross-stitch, so they went out to Daniel's granary and ripped up some grain-bags, in order to get the thread with which they were sewed, to work one apron in cross-stitch.

But when we were ready to sew we were dismayed, for there was no machine. Mrs. O'Shaughnessy, however, was of the opinion that *some one* in the country must have a sewing machine, so she saddled a horse and went out, she said, to "beat the brush."

She was hardly out of sight before a man rode up and said there had been a telephone message saying that Mrs. Holt had arrived in Rock Springs, and was on her way as far as Newfork in an automobile. That threw Elizabeth and myself into a panic. We posted the messenger off on a hunt for Daniel. Elizabeth soon got over her flurry and went at her cross-stitching. I hardly knew what to do, but acting from force of habit, I reckon, I began cleaning. A powerfully good way to reason out things sometimes is to work ; and just then I had to work. I began on the storeroom, which was well lighted and which was also used as a pantry. As soon as I began straightening up I began to wonder where the mother would sleep. By arranging things in the storeroom a little differently, I was able to make room for a bed and a trunk. I decided on putting Daniel there ; so then I began work in earnest. Elizabeth laid down her work and helped me. We tacked white cheesecloth over the wall, and although the floor was clean, we scrubbed it to freshen it. We polished the window until it sparkled. We were right in the middle of our work when Mrs. O'Shaughnessy came, and Daniel with her.

They were all excitement, but Mrs. O'-Shaughnessy is a real general and soon marshaled her forces. Daniel had to go to New-fork after his mother ; that would take three days. Mrs. O'Shaughnessy pointed out to

66

him the need of a few pieces of furniture; so he took a wagon and team, which he got a neighbor to drive, while he took another team and a buggy for his mother. Newfork is a day's drive beyond Pinedale, and the necessary furniture could be had in Pinedale; so the neighbor went along and brought back a new bed, a rocker, and some rugs. But of course he had to stay overnight. I was for keeping right on house-cleaning; but as Mrs. O'Shaughnessy had arranged for us all to come and sew that afternoon at a near-by house, we took our sewing and clambered into the buckboard and set out.

We found Mrs. Bonham a pleasant little woman whose husband had earned her pretty new machine by chewing tobacco. I reckon you think that is a mighty funny method of earning anything, but some tobacco has tags which are redeemable, and the machine was one of the premiums. Mrs. Bonham just beamed with pride as she rolled out her machine. "I never had a machine before," she

67

explained. "I just went to the neighbors'
when I had to sew. So of course I wanted a
machine awfully bad. So Frank jest chawed
and chawed, and I saved every tag till we
got enough, and last year we got the machine. Frank is chawin' out a clock now; but
that won't take him so long as the machine
did."

Well, the "chawed-out" machine did splen-
didly, and we turned out some good work
that afternoon. I completed the blue bonnet
which was to be used as "best," and made
a "splint" bonnet. Mrs. O'Shaughnessy and
Elizabeth did well on their aprons. We took
turn about at the machine and not a minute
was wasted. Mrs. Bonham showed us some
crochet lace which she said she hoped to sell;
and right at once Mrs. O'Shaughnessy's fer-
tile mind begin to hatch plans. She would
make Mrs. Holt a "Sunday apron," she said,
and she bought the lace to trim it with. I
thought Mrs. Holt must be an old-fashioned
lady who liked pillow-shams. Mrs. Bonham

had a pretty pair she was willing to sell. On one was worked, " Good Morning "; on the other, "Good Night"; it was done with red cotton. The shams had a dainty edge of homemade lace. Elizabeth would not be outdone; she purchased a star quilt pieced in red and white. At sundown we went home. We were all tired, but as soon as supper was over we went to work again. We took down the bed and set it up in Dan's new quarters, and we made such headway on what had been his bedroom that we knew we could finish in a little while next day.

The next morning, as soon as we had breakfasted, Mrs. O'Shaughnessy and Elizabeth went back to sew, taking with them a lot of white cheesecloth for lining for the bedroom we were preparing for Mrs. Holt. Mr. Stewart had had fine luck fishing, but he said he felt plumb left out with so much bustling about and he not helping. He is very handy with a saw and hammer, and he contrived what we called a "chist of drawers," for Daniel's room.

# LETTERS ON AN ELK HUNT

The "chist" had only one drawer; into that we put all the gloves, ties, handkerchiefs, and suspenders, and on the shelves below we put his shoes and boots. Then I made a blue curtain for the "chist" and one for the window, and the room looked plumb nice, I can tell you. I liked the "chist" so well that I asked Mr. Stewart to make something of the kind for Mrs. Holt's room. He said there would n't be time, but he went to work on it.

Promptly at noon Mrs. O'Shaughnessy and Elizabeth came with the lining for the room. We worked like beavers, and had the room sweet and ready by mid-afternoon, when the man came from Pinedale with the new furniture. In just a little while we had the room in perfect order: the bed nicely made with soft, new blankets for sheets; the pretty star quilt on, and the nice, clean pillows protected by the shams. They could buy no rugs, but a weaver of rag carpets in Pinedale had some pieces of carpet which Daniel sent back to us. They were really better and greatly more in

## DANYUL AND HIS MOTHER

keeping. We were very proud of the pretty white and red room when we were through. Only the kitchen was left, but we decided we could clean that early next day; so we sat down to sew and to plan the next day's dinner. We could hear Mr. Stewart out in the barn hammering and sawing on the "chist."

While we were debating whether to have fried chicken or trout for dinner, two little girls, both on one horse, rode up. They entered shyly, and after carefully explaining to us that they had heard that a wagon-load of women were buying everything they could see, had run Mr. Holt off, and were living in his house, they told us they had come to sell us some blueing. When they got two dollars' worth sold, the blueing company would send them a big doll; so, please, would we buy a lot?

We did n't think we could use any blueing, but we hated to disappoint the little things. We talked along, and presently they told us of their mother's flowers. Daniel had told us his mother *always* had a red flower in her kitchen window. When the little girls assured us their mother had a red geranium in bloom, Mrs. O'Shaughnessy set out to get it; and about dark she returned with a beautiful plant just beginning to bloom. We were all as happy as children; we had all worked very hard, too. Mr. Stewart said we deserved no sympathy because we cleaned a perfectly clean house; but, anyway, we felt much better for having gone over it.

The "chist" was finished early next morning. It would have looked better, perhaps, if it had had a little paint, but as we had no paint and were short of time, we persuaded ourselves it looked beautiful with only its clean, pretty curtain. We did n't make many changes in the kitchen. All we did was to take down the mirror and turn it lengthways above the mantel-shelf over the fireplace. We put the new rocker in the bright, sunny corner, where it would be easier for dim old eyes to see to read or sew. We set the geranium on the broad clean sill of the window, and I think you would have agreed with us that it was a cozy, cheerful home to come to after fifteen years of lonely homelessness. We could n't get the dinner question settled, so we "dished in dirty-face"; each cooked what she thought best. Like Samantha Ann Allen, we had "everything good and plenty of it."

Elizabeth took a real interest and worked well. She is the *dearest* girl and would be a precious daughter to some mother. She has not yet told us anything about herself. All we know is, she taught school somewhere in the East. She was a little surprised at the way we took possession of a stranger's home, but she enjoyed it as much as we. "It is so nice to be doing something for some one again, something real homey and family-like," she remarked as she laid the table for dinner.

We had dinner almost ready when we heard the wheels crossing the mossy log bridge. We raced to let down the bars. Beside Daniel sat a dear dumpy little woman, her head very much bundled up with a lot of old black

73

veils. Daniel drove through the corral, into
the yard, and right up to the door. He
helped her out *so* gently. She kept admonishing him, "Careful, Danyul, careful." He
handed out her crutch and helped her into
the kitchen, where she sank, panting, into the
rocker. "It is my leg," she explained; "it has
been that way ever since Danyul was a baby."
Then she pleaded, "Careful, careful," to Elizabeth, who was tenderly unwrapping her. "I
would n't have anything happen to this brown
alapacky for anything; it is my very best, and
I've had it ever since before I went to the pore
farm; but I wanted to look nice for Danyul,
comin' to his home for the first time an' all."

We had the happiest dinner party I ever
remember. It would be powerfully hard for
me to say which was happier, "Danyul" or his
mother. They just beamed upon each other.
She was proud of her boy and his pleasant
home. "Danyul says he's got a little red
heifer for me and he's got ten cows of his own.
Now ain't that fine? It is a pity we can't have

# DANYUL AND HIS MOTHER

a few apple trees, — a little orchard. We'd
live like kings, we would that." We explained
to her how we got our fruit by parcel post, and
Danyul said he would order his winter supply
of apples at once.

As soon as dinner was over, Danyul had to
mend a fence so as to keep his cattle in their
own pasture. Mr. Stewart went to help and
we women were left alone. We improved the
time well. Mrs. Holt would not lie down and
rest, as we tried to persuade her to, but hobbled about, admiring everything. She was
delighted with the big, clean cellar and its
orderly bins, in which Danyul was beginning
to store his vegetables. She was as pleased as
a child with her room, and almost wept when
we told her which were "welcoming presents"
from us. She was particularly delighted with
her red flower, and Mrs. O'Shaughnessy will
be happy for days remembering it was she
who gave it. I shall be happy longer than
that remembering how tickled she was with
her bonnets.

75

# LETTERS ON AN ELK HUNT

She wanted to wipe the dishes, so she and I did up the dishes while Mrs. O'Shaughnessy and Elizabeth put some finishing stitches in on their aprons. She sat on the highest seat we could find, and as she deftly handled the dishes she told us this : —

"I should think you would wonder why Danyul ain't got me out of the porehouse before now. I've been there more 'n ten years, but Danyul did n't know it till a month ago. Charlotte Nash wrote him. Neither Danyul nor me are any master-hand at writin', and then I did n't want him to know anyhow. When Danyul got into trouble, I signed over the little farm his pa left us, to pay the lawyer person to defend him. Danyul had enough trouble, so he went to the penitentiary without finding out I was homeless. I should think you would be put out to know Danyul has been to the pen, but he has. He always said to me that he never done what he was accused of, so I am not going to tell you what it was. Danyul was always a good boy, honest and good to me

76

and a hard worker. I ain't got no call to doubt him when he says he 's innocent.

"Well, I fought his case the best I could, but he got ten years. Then the lawyer person claimed the home an' all, so I went out to work, but bein' crippled I found it hard. When Danyul had been gone four years I had saved enough to buy my brown alapacky and go to see him. He looked pale and sad, —afraid even to speak to his own mother. I went back to work as broke up as Danyul, and that winter I come down with such a long spell of sickness that they sent me to the pore farm. I always wrote to Danyul on his birthday and I could n't bear to let him know where I was.

"Soon 's his time was out, he come here; he could n't bear the scorn that he 'd get at home, so he come out to this big, free West, and took the chance it offers. Once he wrote and asked me if I would like to live West. He said if I did, after he got a start I must sell out and come to him. Bless his heart, all that time I was going to my meals just when I was told to and eatin' just what I was helped to, going to bed and getting up at some one else's word! Oh, it was bitter, but I did n't want Danyul to taste it; so, when I did n't come, he thought I did n't want to give up the old home, and did n't say no more about it. Charlotte was on the pore farm too, until her cousin died and she got left a home and enough to live on. Sometimes she would come out to the farm and take me back with her for a little visit. She was good that way. I never would tell her about Danyul; but this summer I was helpin' her dry apples and somehow she jist coaxed the secret out. She wrote to Danyul, and he wrote to me, and here I am. Danyul and me are so happy that we are goin' to send a ticket back to the farm for Maggie Harper. She ain't got no home and will be glad to help me and get a rale home."

Mrs. O'Shaughnessy and Elizabeth debated what more was needed to make the kitchen

# DANYUL AND HIS MOTHER

a bit more homey. Mrs. O'Shaughnessy said
a red cushion for the rocker, and Elizabeth
said a white cat to lie on the hearth. Mrs.
Holt said, "Yes, I *do* need 'em both, —
only it must be an old stray tabby cat. This
house is going to be the shelter of the homeless."

Well, I can't tell you any more about the
Holts because we left next morning. Danyul
came across the bridge to bid us good-bye.
He said he could never thank us enough, but
it is we who should be and are thankful. We
got a little glow of happiness from their great
blaze. We are all so glad to know that everything is secure and bright for the Holts in
the future.

That stop is the cause of my missing two
letters to you, but this letter is as long as half
a dozen letters should be. You know I never
could get along with few words. I'll try to
do better next time. But I can't imagine how
I shall get the letters mailed. We are miles
and miles and miles away in the mountains;

## LETTERS ON AN ELK HUNT

it is two days' ride to a post-office, so maybe I will not get letters to you as often as I planned.

Sincerely yours,

ELINORE RUPERT STEWART.

# VI

## ELIZABETH'S ROMANCE

DEAR MRS. CONEY, —

I find I can't write to you as often as I at
first intended; but I've a chance to-day, so
I will not let it pass unused. We are in the
last camp, right on the hunting ground, in
the "midst of the fray." We have said good-
bye to dear Elizabeth, and I must tell you
about her because she really comes first.

To begin with, the morning we left the
Holts, Elizabeth suggested that we three
women ride in the buckboard, so I seated
myself on a roll of bedding in the back part.
At first none of us talked; we just absorbed
the wonderful green-gold beauty of the morning. The sky was clear blue, with a few fleecy
clouds drifting lazily past. The mountains on

81

one side were crested; great crags and piles
of rock crowned them as far as we could see;
timber grew only about halfway up. The
trunks of the quaking aspens shone silvery
in the early sunlight, and their leaves were
shimmering gold. And the stately pines kept
whispering and murmuring; it almost seemed
as if they were chiding the quaking aspens
for being frivolous. On the other side of the
road lay the river, bordered by willows and
grassy flats. There were many small lakes,
and the ducks and geese were noisily enjoy-
ing themselves among the rushes and water-
grasses. Beyond the river rose the forest-
covered mountains, hill upon hill.

Elizabeth dressed with especial care that
morning, and very pretty she looked in her
neat shepherd's plaid suit and natty little
white canvas hat. Very soon she said, "I
hope neither of you will misunderstand me
when I tell you that if my hopes are realized
I will not ride with you much longer. I never
saw such a country as the West, — it is so

## ELIZABETH'S ROMANCE

big and so beautiful, — and I never saw such people. You are just like your country; you have fed me, cared for me, and befriended me, a stranger, and never asked me a word."

Mrs. O'Shaughnessy said, "Tut, tut, 't is nothing at all we 've done. 'T is a comfort you 've been, has n't she, Mrs. Stewart?"

I could heartily agree ; and Elizabeth went on, "The way I have been received and the way we all treated Mrs. Holt will be the greatest help to me in becoming what I hope to become, a real Westerner. I might have lived a long time in the West and not have understood many things if I had not fallen into your hands. Years ago, before I was through school, I was to have been married ; but I lost my mother just then and was left the care of my paralytic father. If I had married then, I should have had to take father from his familiar surroundings, because Wallace came West in the forestry service. I felt that it would n't be right. Poor father could n't speak, but his eyes told me how grateful he was to stay. We had our little home and father had his pension, and I was able to get a small school near us. I could take care of father and teach also. We were very comfortably situated, and in time became really happy. Although I seldom heard from Wallace, his letters were well worth waiting for, and I knew he was doing well.

"Eighteen months ago father died, — gently went to sleep. I waited six months and then wrote to Wallace, but received no reply. I have written him three times and have had no word. I could bear it no longer and have come to see what has become of him. If he is dead, may I stay on with one of you and perhaps get a school? I want to live here always."

"But, darlint," said Mrs. O'Shaughnessy, "supposin' it's married your man is?"

"Wallace may have changed his mind about me, but he would not marry without telling me. If he is alive he is honorable."

Then I asked, "Why did n't you ask about

him at Pinedale or any of these places we have passed? If he is stationed in the Bridges reserve they would be sure to know of him at any of these little places."

"I just didn't have the courage to. I should never have told you what I have, only I think I owe it to you, and it was easier because of the Holts. I am so glad we met them."

So we drove along, talking together; we each assured the girl of our entire willingness to have her as a member of the family. After a while I got on to the wagon with Mr. Stewart and told him Elizabeth's story so that he could inquire about the man. Soon we came to the crossing on Green River. Just beyond the ford we could see the game-warden's cabin, with the stars and stripes fluttering gayly in the fresh morning breeze. We drove into the roaring, dashing water, and we held our breath until we emerged on the other side.

Mr. Sorenson is a very capable and conscientious game-warden and a very genial gentleman. He rode down to meet us, to inspect our license and to tell us about our privileges and our duties as good woodsmen. He also issues licenses in case hunters have neglected to secure them before coming. Mrs. O'Shaughnessy had refused to get a license when we did. She said she was not going to hunt; she told us we could give her a small piece of "ilk" and that would do; so we were rather surprised when she purchased two licenses, one a special, which would entitle her to a bull elk. As we were starting Mr. Stewart asked the game-warden, " Can you tell me if Wallace White is still stationed here?" "Oh, yes," Mr. Sorenson said, " Wallace's place is only a few miles up the river and can be plainly seen from the road."

We drove on. Happiness had taken a new clutch upon my heart. I looked back, expecting to see Elizabeth all smiles, but if you will believe me the foolish girl was sobbing as if her heart was broken. Mrs. O'Shaughnessy drew her head down upon her shoulder and was trying to quiet her. The road along there

86

was *very* rough. Staying on the wagon oc-
cupied all my attention for a while. Several
miles were passed when we came in sight of
a beautiful cabin, half hidden in a grove of
pines beyond the river. Mr. Stewart said we
might as well "noon" as soon as we came to
a good place, and then he would ride across
and see Mr. White.

Just as we rounded the hill a horseman
came toward us. A splendid fellow he was,
manly strength and grace showing in every
line. The road was narrow against the hillside
and he had to ride quite close, so I saw his
handsome face plainly. As soon as he saw
Elizabeth he sprang from his saddle and said,
"'Liz'beth, 'Liz'beth, what you doin' here?"

She held her hands to him and said, "Oh,
just riding with friends." Then to Mrs.
O'Shaughnessy she said, "*This* is my Wallace."

Mr. Stewart is the queerest man: instead
of letting me enjoy the tableau, he solemnly
drove on, saying he would not want any one

87

gawking at him if he were the happy man.
Anyway, he could n't urge Chub fast enough
to prevent my seeing and hearing what I've
told you. Besides that, I saw that Elizabeth's
hat was on awry, her hair in disorder, and her
eyes red. It was disappointing after she had
been so careful to look nicely.

Mrs. O'Shaughnessy came trotting along
and we stopped for dinner. We had just got
the coffee boiling when the lovers came up,
Elizabeth in the saddle, "learning to ride,"
and he walking beside her holding her hand.
How happy they were! The rest of us were
mighty near as foolish as they. They were
going to start immediately after dinner, on
horseback, for the county seat, to be married.
After we had eaten, Elizabeth selected a few
things from her trunk, and Mr. Stewart and
Mr. White drove the buckboard across the
river to leave the trunk in its new home.
While they were gone we helped Elizabeth to
dress. All the while Mrs. O'Shaughnessy was
admonishing her to name her first "girul"

## ELIZABETH'S ROMANCE

Mary Ellen; "or," she said, "if yer first girul happens to be a b'y, it's Sheridan ye'll be callin' him, which was me name before I was married to me man, God rest his soul."

Dear Elizabeth, she was glad to get away, I suspect! She and her Wallace made a fine couple as they rode away in the golden September afternoon. I believe she is *one* happy bride that the sun shone on, if the omen has failed *everywhere* else.

Well, we felt powerfully reduced in numbers, but about three o'clock that afternoon we came upon Mr. Struble and Mr. Haynes waiting beside the road for us. They had come to pilot us into camp, for there would be no road soon.

Such a way as we came over! Such jolting and sliding! I begged to get off and walk; but as the whole way was carpeted by strawberry vines and there were late berries to tempt me to loiter, I had to stay on the wagon. I had no idea a wagon could be got across such places.

89

# LETTERS ON AN ELK HUNT

Mr. Struble drove for Mrs. O'Shaughnessy, and I could hear her imploring all the saints to preserve us from instant death. I kept shutting my eyes, trying not to see the terrifying places, and opening them again to see the beauty spread everywhere, until Mr. Stewart said, "It must make you nervous to ride over mountain roads. Don't bat your eyes so fast and you'll see more." So then I stiffened my back and kept my eyes open, and I *did* see more.

It had been decided to go as far as we could with the wagons and then set camp; from there the hunters would ride horseback as far up as they could and then climb. It was almost sundown when we reached camp. All the hunters were in, and such a yowling as they set up! "Look who's here! See who's come!" they yelled. They went to work setting up tents and unloading wagons with a hearty good-will.

We are camped just on the edge of the pines. Back of us rises a big pine-clad mountain; our tents are set under some big trees, on a small plateau, and right below us is a valley in which grass grows knee high and little streams come from every way. Trout scurry up stream whenever we go near. We call the valley Paradise Valley because it is the horses' paradise. And as in the early morning we can often see clouds rolling along the valley, we call our camp Cloud-crest. We have a beautiful place: it is well sheltered; there is plenty of wood, water, and feed; and, looking eastward down the valley, snow-covered, crag-topped mountains delight the eye.

The air is so bracing that we all feel equal to *anything*. Mr. Struble has already killed a fine "spike" elk for camp eating. We camped in a bunch, and we have camp stoves so that in case of rain or snow we can stay indoors. Just now we have a huge camp fire around which we sit in the evening, telling stories, singing, and eating nuts of the piñon pine. Then too the whole country is filled with those tiny little strawberries. We have to gather all day to get as much as we can eat, but they are delicious. Yesterday we had pie made of wild currants; there are a powerful lot of them here. There is also a little blueberry that the men say is the Rocky Mountain huckleberry. The grouse are feeding on them. Altogether this is one of the most delightful places imaginable. The men are not very anxious to begin hunting. A little delay means cooler weather for the meat. It is cool up here, but going back across the desert it will be warm for a while yet. Still, when they see elk every day it is a great temptation to try a shot.

One of the students told me Professor Glenholdt was here to get the tip-end bone of the tail of a brontosaurus. I don't know what that is, but if it is a fossil he won't get it, for the soil is too deep. The students are jolly, likable fellows, but they can talk of nothing but strata and formation. I heard one of them say he would be glad when some one killed a bear, as he had heard they were fine eating, having strata of fat alternating with strata of lean. Mr. Haynes is a quiet fellow, just interested in hunting. Mr. Struble is the big man of the party; he is tall and strong and we find him very pleasant company. Then there is Dr. Teschall; he is a quiet fellow with an unexpected smile. He is so reserved that I felt that he was kind of out of place among the rest until I caught his cordial smile. He is so slight that I don't see how he will stand the hard climbing, not to mention carrying the heavy gun. They are using the largest caliber sporting guns, — murderous-looking things. That is, all except Mr. Harkrudder, the picture man. He looks to be about forty years old, but whoops and laughs like he was about ten.

I don't need to tell you of the "good mon," do I? He is just the kind, quiet good mon that he has always been since I have known him. A young lady from a neighboring camp came over and said she had called to see our *tout ensemble.* Well, I 've given you it, they, us, or we.

We did n't need a guide, as Mr. Haynes and Mr. Struble are old-timers. We were to have had a cook, but when we reached Pine-dale, where we were to have picked him up, he told Mr. Haynes he was "too tam seek in de bel," so we had to come without him ; but that is really no inconvenience, since we are all very good cooks and are all willing to help. I don't think I shall be able to tell you of any great exploits I make with the gun. I fired one that Mr. Stewart carries, and it almost kicked my shoulder off. I am mysti-fied about Mrs. O'Shaughnessy's license. I know she would not shoot one of those big guns for a dozen elk; besides that, she is very tender-hearted and will never harm any-thing herself, although she likes to join our hunts.

I think you must be tired of this letter, so I am going to say good-night, my friend.

E. R. S.

# VII

## THE HUNT

DEAR MRS. CONEY, —

It seems so odd to be writing you and getting no answers. Mrs. O'Shaughnessy just now asked me what I have against you that I write you so much. I have n't one thing. I told her I owed you more love than I could ever pay in a lifetime, and she said writing such *long* letters is a mighty poor way to show it. I have been neglecting you shamefully, I think. One of the main reasons I came on this hunt was to take the trip for *you*, and to tell you things that you would most enjoy. So I will spend this snowy day in writing to you.

On the night of September 30, there was the most awful thunderstorm I ever witnessed, — flash after flash of the most blind-

95

ing lightning, followed by deafening peals of thunder; and as it echoed from mountain to mountain the uproar was terrifying. I have always loved a storm; the beat of hail and rain, and the roar of wind always appeal to me; but there was neither wind nor rain, — just flash and roar. Before the echo died away among the hills another booming report would seem to shiver the atmosphere and set all our tinware jangling. We are camped so near the great pines that I will confess I was powerfully afraid. Had the lightning struck one of the big pines there would not have been one of us left. I could hear Mrs. O'- Shaughnessy murmuring her prayers when there was a lull. We had gone to bed, but I could n't remain there; so I sat on the wagon- seat with Jerrine beside me. Something struck the guy ropes of the tent, and I was so fright- ened I was too weak to cry out. I thought the big tree must have fallen. In the lulls of the storm I could hear the men's voices, high and excited. They, too, were up. It seemed

# THE HUNT

to me that the storm lasted for hours; but at last it moved off up the valley, the flashes grew to be a mere glimmer, and the thunder mere rumbling. The pines began to moan, and soon a little breeze whistled by. So we lay down again. Next morning the horses could not be found; the storm had frightened them, and they had tried to go home. The men had to find them, and as it took most of the day, we had to put off our hunt.

We were up and about next morning in the first faint gray light. While the men fed grain to the horses and saddled them, we prepared a hasty breakfast. We were off before it was more than light enough for us to see the trail.

Dawn in the mountains — how I wish I could describe it to you! If I could only make you feel the keen, bracing air, the exhilarating climb; if I could only paint its beauties, what a picture you should have! Here the colors are very different from those of the desert. I suppose the forest makes it

so. The shadows are mellow, like the colors
in an old picture— greenish amber light and
a blue-gray sky. Far ahead of us we could
see the red rim rock of a mountain above
timber line. The first rays of the sun turned
the jagged peaks into golden points of a
crown. In Oklahoma, at that hour of the day,
the woods would be alive with song-birds,
even at this season; but here there are no
song-birds, and only the snapping of twigs,
as our horses climbed the frosty trail, broke
the silence. We had been cautioned not to
talk, but neither Mrs. O'Shaughnessy nor I
wanted to. Afterwards, when we compared
notes, we found that we both had the same
thought: we both felt ashamed to be out to
deal death to one of the Maker's beautiful
creatures, and we were planning how we
might avoid it.

The sun was well up when we reached the
little park where we picketed our horses.
Then came a long, hard climb. It is hard
climbing at the best, and when there is a big

# THE HUNT

gun to carry, it is *very* hard. Then too, we had to keep up with the men, and we did n't find that easy to do. At last we reached the top and sat down on some boulders to rest a few minutes before we started down to the hunting ground, which lay in a cuplike valley far below us.

We could hear the roar of the Gros Ventre as it tumbled grumbingly over its rocky bed. To our right rose mile after mile of red cliffs. As the last of the quaking asp leaves have fallen, there were no golden groves. In their places stood silvery patches against the red background of the cliffs. High overhead a triangle of wild geese harrowed the blue sky.

I was plumb out of breath, but men who are most gallant elsewhere are absolutely heartless on a hunt. I was scarcely through panting before we began to descend. We received instructions as to how we should move so as to keep out of range of each other's guns ; then Mr. Haynes and myself started one way, and Mr. Struble and Mrs. O'Shaugh-

LETTERS ON AN ELK HUNT

nessy the other. We were to meet where the valley terminated in a broad pass. We felt sure we could get a chance at what elk there might be in the valley. We were following fresh tracks, and a little of the hunter's enthusiasm seized me.

We had not followed them far when three cows and a "spike" came running out of the pines a little ahead of us. Instantly Mr. Haynes's gun flew to his shoulder and a deafening report jarred our ears. He ran forward, but I stood still, fascinated by what I saw. Our side of the valley was bounded by a rim of rock. Over the rim was a sheer wall of rock for two hundred feet, to where the Gros Ventre was angrily roaring below; on the other side of the stream rose the red cliffs with their jagged crags. At the report of the gun two huge blocks of stone almost as large as a house detached themselves and fell. At the same instant one of the quaking asp groves began to move slowly. I could n't believe my eyes. I shut them a moment, but

# THE HUNT

when I looked the grove was moving faster. It slid swiftly, and I could plainly hear the rattle of stones falling against stones, until with a muffled roar the whole hillside fell into the stream.

Mr. Haynes came running back. "What is the matter? Are you hurt? Why did n't you shoot?" he asked.

I waved my hand weakly toward where the great mound of tangled trees and earth blocked the water. "Why," he said, "that is only a landslide, not an earthquake. You are as white as a ghost. Come on up here and see my fine elk."

I sat on a log watching him dress his elk. We have found it best not to remove the skin, but the elk have to be quartered so as to load them on to a horse. Mrs. O'Shaughnessy and Mr. Struble came out of the woods just then. They had seen a big bunch of elk headed by a splendid bull, but got no shot, and the elk went out of the pass. They had heard our shot, and came across to see what luck.

# LETTERS ON AN ELK HUNT

"What iver is the matter with ye?" asked Mrs. O'Shaughnessy. Mr. Haynes told her. They had heard the noise, but had thought it thunder. Mr. Haynes told me that if I would "chirk up" he would give me his elk teeth. Though I don't admire them, they are considered valuable; however, his elk was a cow, and they don't have as nice teeth as do bulls.

We had lunch, and the men covered the elk with pine boughs to keep the camp robbers from pecking it full of holes. Next day the men would come with the horses and pack it in to camp. We all felt refreshed; so we started on the trail of those that got away.

For a while walking was easy and we made pretty good time; then we had a rocky hill to get over. We had to use care when we got into the timber; there were marshy places which tried us sorely, and windfall so thick that we could hardly get through. We were obliged to pick our way carefully to avoid noise, and we were all together, not having

# THE HUNT

come to a place where it seemed better to separate. We had about resolved to go to our horses when we heard a volley of shots.

"That is somebody bunch-shooting," said Mr. Struble. "They are in Brewster Lake Park, by the sound. That means that the elk will pass here in a short time and we may get a shot. The elk will be here long before the men, since the men have no horses; so let's hurry and get placed along the only place they can get out. We'll get our limit.

We hastily secreted ourselves along the narrow gorge through which the elk must pass. We were all on one side, and Mr. Haynes said to me, "Rest your gun on that rock and aim at the first rib back of the shoulder. If you shoot haphazard you may cripple an elk and let it get away to die in misery. So make sure when you fire."

It did n't seem a minute before we heard the beat of their hoofs and a queer panting noise that I can't describe. First came a beautiful thing with his head held high; his great antlers seemed to lie half his length on his back; his eyes were startled, and his shining black mane seemed to bristle. I heard the report of guns, and he tumbled in a confused heap. He tried to rise, but others coming leaped over him and knocked him down. Some more shots, and those behind turned and went back the way they had come.

Mr. Haynes shouted to me, "Shoot, shoot; why *don't* you shoot!"

So I fired my Krag, but next I found myself picking myself up and wondering who had struck me and for what. I was so dizzy I could scarcely move, but I got down to where the others were excitedly admiring the two dead elk that they said were the victims of Mrs. O'Shaughnessy's gun. She was as excited and delighted as if she had never declared she would not kill anything. "Sure, it's many a meal they'll make for little hungry mouths," she said. She was rubbing her shoulder ruefully. "I don't want to fire any more big guns. I thought old Goliar had hit

# THE HUNT

me a biff with a blackthorn shilaley," she remarked.

Mr. Haynes turned to me and said, "You
are a dandy hunter! you did n't shoot at all
until after the elk were gone, and the way
you held your gun it is a wonder it did n't
knock your head off, instead of just smashing
your jaw."

The men worked as fast as they could at
the elk, and we helped as much as we could,
but it was dark before we reached camp. Supper was ready, but I went to bed at once.
They all thought it was because I was so dis-
appointed, but it was because I was so stiff
and sore I could hardly move, and so tired I
could n't sleep. Next morning my jaw and
neck were so swollen that I hated any one to
see me, and my head ached for two days. It
has been snowing for a long time, but Clyde
says he will take me hunting when it stops. I
don't want to go but reckon I will have to, because I don't want to come so far and buy a
license to kill an elk and go back empty-

handed, and partly to get a rest from Mr. Murry's everlasting accordion.

Mr. Murry is an old-time acquaintance of Mrs. O'Shaughnessy's. He has a ranch down on the river somewhere. Mrs. O'Shaughnessy has not seen him for years, — did n't know he lived up here. He had seen the game-warden from whom she had procured her license, and so hunted up our camp. He is an odd-looking individual, with sad eyes and a drooping mouth which gives his face a most hopeless, reproachful expression. His nose, however, seems to upset the original plan, for it is long and thin and bent slightly to one side. His neck is long and his Adam's apple seems uncertain as to where it belongs. At supper Jerrine watched it as if fascinated until I sent her from the table and went out to speak to her about gazing.

"Why, mamma," she said, "I had to look; he has swallowed something that won't go either up or down, and I 'm 'fraid he 'll choke."

# THE HUNT

Although I can't brag about Mr. Murry's appearance, I can about his taste, for he admires Mrs. O'Shaughnessy. It seems that in years gone by he has made attempts to marry her.

As he got up from supper the first night he was with us, he said, "Mary Ellen, I have a real treat and surprise for you. Just wait a few minutes, an' I 'll bet you 'll be happy."

We took our accustomed places around the fire, while Mr. Murry hobbled his cayuse and took an odd-looking bundle from his saddle. He seated himself and took from the bundle—an accordion! He set it upon his knee and began pulling and pushing on it. He did what Mr. Struble said was doling a doleful tune. Every one took it good-naturedly, but he kept doling the doleful until little by little the circle thinned.

Our tent is as comfortable as can be. Now that it is snowing, we sit around the stoves, and we should have fine times if Professor Glenholt could have a chance to talk ; but we have

LETTERS ON AN ELK HUNT

to listen to "Run, Nigger, Run" and "The Old Gray Hoss Come A-tearin' Out The Wilderness." I'll sing them to you when I come to Denver.

With much love to you,

ELINORE RUPERT STEWART.

# VIII

## THE SEVENTH MAN

CLOUDCREST, October 10, 1914.

DEAR MRS. CONEY, —

I wonder what you would do if you were
here. But I reckon I had better not anticipate,
and so I will begin at the beginning. On the
morning of the eighth we held a council.
The physician and the two students had
gone. All had their limit of elk except Mr.
Haynes and myself. Our licenses also entitled each of us to a deer, a mountain sheep,
and a bear. We had plenty of food, but it
had snowed about a foot and I was beginning to want to get out while the going was
good. Two other outfits had gone out. The
doctor and the students hired them to haul
out their game. So we decided to stay on a
week longer.

That morning Mrs. O'Shaughnessy and I

melted snow and washed the clothes. It was delightful to have nice soft water, and we enjoyed our work; it was almost noon before we thought to begin dinner. I suppose you would say lunch, but with us it is dinner. None of the men had gone out that day.

Mr. Harkrudder was busy with his films and did n't come with the rest when dinner was ready. When he did come, he was excited; he laid a picture on the table and said, "Do any of you recognize this?"

It looked like a flash-light of our camping ground. It was a little blurry, but some of the objects were quite clear. Our tent was a white blotch except for the outlines; the wagons showed plainly. I did n't think much of it as a picture, so I paid scant attention. Mrs. O'Shaughnessy gave it close scrutiny; presently she said, "Oh, yis, I see what it is. It 's a puzzle picture and ye find the man. Here he is, hidin' beyont the pine next the tent."

"Exactly," said Harkrudder, "but I had not expected just this. I am working out

## THE SEVENTH MAN

some ideas of my own in photography, and this picture is one of the experiments I tried the night of the storm. The result does n't prove my experiment either way. Where were you, Stewart, during the storm?"

"Where should I be? I bided i' the bed," the Stewart said.

"Well," said Harkrudder, "I know where each of the other fellows was, and none of them was in this direction. Now who is the seventh man?"

I looked again, and, sure enough, there was a man in a crouching position outlined against the tent wall. We were all excited, for it was ten minutes past one when Harkrudder was out, and we could n't think why any one would be prowling about our camp at that time of the night.

As Mr. Stewart and I had planned a long, beautiful ride, we set out after dinner, leaving the rest yet at the table eating and conjecturing about the "stranger within our picture." I had hoped we would come to ground level enough for a sharp, invigorating canter, but our way was too rough. It was a joy to be out in the great, silent forest. The snow made riding a little venturesome because the horses slipped a great deal, but Chub is dependable even though he *is* lazy. Clyde bestrode Mr. Haynes's Old Blue. We were headed for the cascades on Clear Creek, to see the wonderful ice-caverns that the flying spray is forming.

We had almost reached the cascades and were crossing a little bowl-like valley, when an elk calf leaped out of the snow and ran a few yards. It paused and finally came irresolutely back toward us. A few steps farther we saw great, red splotches on the snow and the body of a cow elk. Around it were the tracks of the faithful little calf. It would stay by its mother until starvation or wild animals put an end to its suffering. The cow was shot in half a dozen places, none of them in a fatal spot; it had bled to death. "That," said Mr. Stewart angrily, "comes o' bunch

# THE SEVENTH MAN

shooting. The authorities should revoke the license of a man found guilty of bunch shooting."

We rode on in silence, each a little saddened by what we had seen. But this was not all. We had begun to descend the mountain side to Clear Creek when we came upon the beaten trail of a herd of elk. We followed it as offering perhaps the safest descent. It did n't take us far. Around the spur of the mountain the herd had stampeded; tracks were everywhere. Lying in the trail were a spike and an old bull with a broken antler. Chub shied, but Old Blue does n't scare, so Mr. Stewart rode up quite close. Around the heads were tell-tale tracks. We did n't dismount, but we knew that the two upper teeth or tushes were missing and that the hated tooth-hunter was at work. The tracks in the snow showed there had been two men. An adult elk averages five hundred pounds of splendid meat; here before us, therefore, lay a thousand pounds of food thrown to waste

113

just to enable a contemptible tooth-hunter to obtain four teeth. Tooth-hunting is against the law, but this is a case where you must catch before hanging.

Well, we saw the cascades, and after resting a little, we started homeward through the heavy woods, where we were compelled to go more slowly. We had dismounted, and were gathering some piñon cones from a fallen tree, when, almost without a sound, a band of elk came trailing down a little draw where a spring trickled. We watched them file along, evidently making for lower ground on which to bed. Chub snorted, and a large cow stopped and looked curiously in our direction. Those behind passed leisurely around her. We knew she had no calf, because she was light in color: cows suckling calves are of a darker shade. A loud report seemed to rend the forest, and the beauty dropped. The rest disappeared so suddenly that if the fine specimen that lay before me had not been proof, it would almost have seemed a dream.

# THE SEVENTH MAN

I had shot the cow elk my license called for.

We took off the head and removed the entrails, then covered our game with pine boughs, to which we tied a red bandanna so as to make it easy to find next day, when the men would come back with a saw to divide it down the back and pack it in. There is an imposing row of game hanging in the pines back of our tent. Supper was ready when we got in. Mr. Haynes had been out also and was very joyful; he got his elk this afternoon. We can start home day after to-morrow. It will take the men all to-morrow to get in the game.

I shall be glad to start. I am getting home-sick, and I have not had a letter or even a card since I have been here. We are hungry for war news, and besides, it is snowing again. Our clothes did n't get dry either; they are frozen to the bush we hung them on. Perhaps they will be snowed under by morning. I can't complain, though, for it is warm and pleasant in our tent. The little camp-stove is glowing. Mrs. O'Shaughnessy is showing Jerrine how to make pigs of potatoes. Calvin and Robert are asleep. The men have all gone to the bachelors' tent to form their plans, all save Mr. Murry, who is "serenading" Mrs. O'Shaughnessy. He is playing "Nelly Gray," and somehow I don't want to laugh at him as I usually do; I can only feel sorry for him.

I can hardly write because my heart is yearning for my little Junior boy at home on the ranch with his grandmother. Dear little Mother Stewart, I feel very tender toward her. Junior is the pride of her heart. She would not allow us to bring him on this trip, so she is at the ranch taking care of my brown-eyed boy. Every one is so good, so kind, and I can do so little to repay. It makes me feel very unworthy. You'll think I have the blues, but I haven't. I just feel humble and chastened. When Mr. Murry pauses I can hear the soft spat, spat of the falling snow on the tent. I will be powerfully glad when we set our faces homeward.

Good-night, dear friend. Angels guard you.

ELINORE STEWART.

# IX

## AN INDIAN CAMP

Cloudcrest, October 13, 1914.

Dear, dear Mrs. Coney, —

This is the very last letter you will receive dated from this camp. We are leaving a few days earlier than we intended and I am pretty badly on the fence. I want to laugh, and really I can hardly keep back the tears. We are leaving sooner than we meant, for rather a good reason. We have n't one bite to eat except elk meat.

After the men had brought into camp the elk we killed the other afternoon, they began to plan a sheep hunt. As sheep do not stay in the woods, the men had to go miles away and above timber line. They decided to take a pack horse and stay all night. I did n't want Mr. Stewart to go because the climbing is very dangerous. No accidents have hap-

pened this year, but last season a man fell
from the crags and was killed; so I tried to
keep the "good mon" at home. But he would
not be persuaded. The love of chase has entered his blood, and it looks to me as if it had
chased reason plumb out of his head. I know
exactly how Samantha felt when Josiah *would*
go to the "pleasure exertion." The bald spot
on the Stewart's head does n't seem to remind
him of years gone by; he is as joyous as a
boy.

It was finally decided to take Mrs. O'Shaughnessy and the children and myself to a neighboring camp about two miles away, as we
did n't like to risk being frightened by a pos-
sible intruder. Sorenson, the game-warden,
was in camp to inspect our game on the 12th,
and he told us he was on the trail of tooth-
hunters and had routed them out on the night
of the storm; but what they could have been
doing in our camp was as much a mystery
to him as to us.

Well, when we were ready to go, Mr. Murry

and the Stewart escorted us. It was a cloudy afternoon and often great flakes of snow fell gently, softly. The snow was already about eighteen inches deep, and it made sheep hunting slippery and dangerous work. On our way we came upon an Indian camp. They were all huddled about a tiny fire; scattered about were their wikiups made of sticks and pine boughs. The Indians were sullen and angry. The game-warden had ordered them back to Fort Washakie, where they belonged. Their squaws had jerked their elk. You may not know what jerked means, so I will explain: it means dried, cured. They had all they were allowed, but for some reason they did n't want to go. Sorenson suspects them of being in with the tooth-hunters and he is narrowing the circle.

At the camp where we were to stay, we found Mrs. Kavanaugh laid up with a sore throat, but she made us welcome. It would be a mighty funny camper who would n't. As soon as the men from the Kavanaugh camp

# AN INDIAN CAMP

heard our men's plans, they were eager to go along. So it ended in us three women being left alone. We said we were not afraid and we tried not to feel so, but after dark we all felt a little timorous. Mrs. Kavanaugh was afraid of the Indians, but I was afraid they would bring Clyde back dead from a fall. We were camped in an old cabin built by the ranger. The Kavanaughs were short of groceries. We cooked our big elk steaks on sticks before an open fire, and we roasted potatoes in the ashes. When our fear wore away, we had a fine time. After a while we lay down on fragrant beds of pine.

We awoke late. The fire was dead upon the hearth and outside the snow was piling up. Mrs. O'Shaughnessy made a rousing fire and managed to jolly us until we had a really happy breakfast hour. About three in the afternoon all the men came trooping in, cold, wet, and hungry. After filling them with venison, hot potatoes, and coffee, we started to our own camp. The men were rather depressed because they had come back empty-handed. The Indians were gone and the snow lay thick over the place where their fire had been; they had left in the night.

When we came to camp, Mr. Struble started to build a fire; but no matches were to be had. Next, the men went to feed grain to their tired horses, but the oats were gone. Mr. Murry sought in vain for his beloved accordion. Mr. Harkrudder was furious when he found his grinding machine was gone. Mrs. O'Shaughnessy made a dash for the grub-box. It was empty. We were dumbfounded. Each of us kept searching and researching and knowing all the while we would find nothing. Mr. Struble is a most cheerful individual, and, as Mrs. O'Shaughnessy says, "is a mighty good fellow even if he *is* Dutch." "The Indians have stolen us out," he said, "but after all they have left us our tents and harness, all our meat, and the road home; so what matter if we *are* a little inconvenienced as to grub? Haynes may cry for sugar, but that won't hurt the rest any.

# AN INDIAN CAMP

I'll saddle and ride over to Scotty's and get enough to last us out."

We knew the Kavanaughs could not help us any, but we grew cheerful in anticipating help from Scotty, who was from Green River and was camped a few miles away. We wanted Mr. Struble to wait until morning, but he said no, it would make breakfast late; so he rode off in the dark. At two o'clock this morning he came in almost frozen, with two small cans of milk and two yeast cakes. As soon as it was light enough to see, the men were at work loading the game and breaking camp. As they are ready now to take down this tent, I will have to finish this letter somewhere else.

# X

## THE TOOTH-HUNTERS

AT SORENSON'S CABIN
ON GREEN RIVER.

WELL, we're here, warmed and fed and in
much better trim bodily and mentally. We
had mishap after mishap coming. First the
Hutton horse, being a bronco, had to act up
when he was hitched up. We had almost more
game than we could haul, but at last we got
started, after the bronco had reared and
pitched as much as he wanted to. There are
a great many springs, — one every few feet
in these mountains, — and the snow hid the
pitfalls and made the ground soft, so that the
wheels cut in and pulling was hard. Then,
too, our horses had had nothing to eat for two
days, the snow being so deep they could n't
get at the grass, hobbled as they were.

We had got perhaps a mile from camp

124

when the leading wagon, with four horses driven by Mr. Haynes, suddenly stopped. The wheels had sunk into the soft banks of a small, ditch-like spring branch. Mr. Stewart had to stay on our wagon to hold the bronco, but all the rest, even Mrs. O'Shaughnessy, gathered around and tried to help. They hitched on a snap team, but not a trace tightened. They did n't want to unload the game in the snow. The men lifted and pried on the wheels. Still the horses would n't budge.

Mr. Haynes is no disciple of Job, but he tried manfully to restrain himself. Turning to Glenholdt, who was offering advice, he said, "You get out. I know what the trouble is : these horses used to belong to a freighter and are used to being cussed. It 's the greatest nuisance in the world for a man to go out where there 's a bunch of women. If these women were n't along I 'd make these horses get out of there."

Mrs. O'Shaughnessy said, "Don't lay your poor driving to the women. If you drive by cussin', then *cuss*. We will stop up our ears."

She threw her apron over her head. I held my fingers in Jerrine's ears, and she stopped my ears, else I might be able to tell you what he said. It was something violent, I know. I could tell by the expression of his face. He had only been doing it a second when those horses walked right out with the wagon as nicely as you please. Mrs. O'Shaughnessy said to Mr. Haynes, "It's a poor cusser you are. Sure, it's no wonder you hesitated to begin. If Danny O'Shaughnessy could n't have sworn better, I'd have had to hilp him."

We got along pretty well after that. Mr. Haynes kept some distance ahead ; but occasionally a bit of " cussin' " came back to us and we knew he was using freighter tactics.

The game-warden lives in a tiny little cabin. The door is so low that I had to stoop to get in. It was quite dark when we got here last night, but Mrs. Sorenson acted as if she was *glad* to see us. I did n't think we could

126

all get in. A row of bunks is built along one side of the cabin. A long tarpaulin covers the bed, and we all got upon this and sat while our hostess prepared our supper. If one of us had stirred we would have been in her way; so there we sat as thick as thieves. When supper was ready six got off their perch and ate; when they were through, six more were made happy.

Mr. Sorenson had caught the tooth-hunters. On the wall hung their deadly guns, with silencers on them to muffle the report. He showed us the teeth he had found in their possession. The warden and his deputy had searched the men and their effects and found no teeth. He had no evidence against them except their unlawful guns, but he knew he had the right men. At last he found their contract to furnish two hundred pair of teeth. It is a trick of such hunters to thrust a knife into the meat of the game they have, and so to make pockets in which they hide the teeth; but these fellows had no such pockets. They jeered at the warden and threatened to kill him, but he kept searching, and presently found the teeth in a pail of lard. He told us all about it as we sat, an eager crowd, on his bed. A warden takes his life in his hands when he goes after such fellows, but Sorenson is not afraid to do it.

The cabin walls are covered with pen-and-ink drawings, the work of the warden's gifted children, — Vina, the pretty eighteen-year-old daughter, and Laurence, the sixteen-year-old son. They never had a lesson in drawing in their lives, but their pictures portray Western life exactly.

The snow is not so deep here as it was at camp, but it is too deep for the horses to get grass. The men were able to get a little grain from the warden; so we will pull out in the morning and try to make it to where we can get groceries. We are quite close to where Elizabeth lives, but we should have to cross the river, and it was dark before we passed her home. I should like to see her but

# THE TOOTH-HUNTERS

won't get a chance to. Mrs. Sorenson says she is very happy. In all this round of exposure the kiddies are as well as can be. Cold, camping, and elk meat agree with them. We are in a tent for the night, and it is so cold the ink is freezing, but the kiddies are snuggled under their blankets as warm as toast. We are to start early in the morning. Good-night, dear friend. I am glad I can take this trip *for* you. You 'd freeze.

ELINORE STEWART.

# XI

## BUDDY AND BABY GIRL

In Camp, October 16, 1914.

DEAR MRS. CONEY, —

The day we left the game-warden's was damp and lowering. It did n't seem it could have one good thing to its credit, but there were several things to be thankful for. One of them was that you were safe at home in your warm, dry apartment. We had hardly passed the great Block buttes when the biggest, wettest flakes of snow began to pelt into our faces. I really like a storm, and the kiddies would have enjoyed the snow; but we had to keep the wagon-sheet tied down to keep the bedding dry, and the kiddies get sick under cover. All the pleasure I might have had was taken away by the fact that we were making a forced drive. We *had* to go. The game-warden had no more than enough food for his family, and no horse feed. Also, the snow was almost as deep there as it had been higher up, so the horses could not graze.

We made it to Cora that day. Here at last was plenty of hay and grain; we restocked our mess-boxes and felt better toward the world. Next day we came on here to New-fork, where we are resting our teams before we start across the desert, which begins just across the creek we are camped on.

We have added two to our party. I know you will be interested to know how it happened, and I can picture the astonishment of our neighbors when we reach home, for our newcomers are to be members of Mrs. O'Shaughnessy's family. ,We had all been sorry we could not visit Elizabeth or "Dan-yul" and his mother. We felt almost as if we were sneaking past them, but we consoled ourselves with promises to see the Burneys and Grandma Mortimer. Yesterday the chil-dren and I were riding with Mrs. O'Shaughnessy in the buckboard. We were trotting merrily along the lane that leads to Newfork, thankful in our hearts to be out of the snow, — for there is no snow here. Just ahead of us two little boys were riding along on their ponies. There was a wire fence on both sides of the lane, and almost at the end of the lane an old cow had her head between the wires and was nibbling the tall dead grass. The larger of the two boys said, "That's old Pendry's cow, and she shan't eat a blade of grass off Dad's meadow."

He rode up to the cow and began beating her with his quirt. That frightened the cow, and as she jerked her head up, the top wire caught her across the top of her neck; she jerked and lunged to free herself, and was cruelly cut by the barbs on the wire. Then he began beating his pony.

The small boy said, "You're a coward an' a fool, Billy Polk. The cow wasn't hurtin' nothin', an' you're just tryin' to show off, beatin' that pony."

## BUDDY AND BABY GIRL

Said the other boy, "Shut up, you beggar, or I'll beat you; an' I'll take them breeches you got on off you, an' you can go without any — they're mine. My ma give 'em to you."

The little fellow's face was scarlet — as much of it as we could see for the freckles — and his eyes were blazing as he replied, "You ain't man enough. I dare you to strike me or to tech my clothes."

Both boys were riding bareback. The small boy slid off his pony's back; the other rode up to him and raised his quirt, but the little one seized him by the leg, and in a jiffy they were in the road fighting like cats. I asked Mrs. O'Shaughnessy to drive on, but she said, "If you are in a hurry you can try walkin'; I'm goin' to referee this scrap."

It looked for a minute as if the small boy would get a severe beating, but by some trick he hurled the other headlong into the green, slimy water that edged the road; then, seizing the quirt and the opportunity at the same

133

time, he belabored Billy without mercy as that individual climbed up the slippery embankment, blubbering and whipped. Still sobbing, he climbed upon his patient pony, which stood waiting, and galloped off down the lane. The other pony followed and the little conqueror was left afoot.

Mrs. O'Shaughnessy was beaming with delight. "Sure, 't was a fine fight, a sight worth coming all this way to see. Ah! but you 're the b'y. 'T is a dollar I 'd be givin' ye, only me purse is in me stockin' —"

"Oh," the boy said quickly, "don't let that stop you. I 'll look off another way."

I don't know if she would have given him the money, for just then some men came into the lane with some cattle and we had to start. The boy got up on the back end of the buckboard and we drove on. We could hear our wagons rumbling along and knew they would soon catch up.

"Where is your home, b'y?" asked Mrs. O'Shaughnessy.

## BUDDY AND BABY GIRL

"Oh, just wherever Aunt Hettie has work,"
he said. "She is at Mr. Tom's now, so I'm
there, too, — me and Baby Girl."

"Where are your folks?" Mrs. O'Shaughnessy went on.

"Ma's dead, an pa's gone to Alasky. I
don't know where my brothers are. Baby
Girl an' me are with Aunt Het, an' that's all
there are of us." He grinned cheerfully in
spite of the fact that one eye was fast closing
and he bore numerous bumps and scratches
on his face and head.

Just then one of the men with the cattle
galloped up and shouted, "Hello!" It was
Mr. Burney! "Where'd you get that kid? I
guess I'll have to get the sheriff after you for
kidnapping Bud. And what have you been
doing to him, anyway?"

Mrs. O'Shaughnessy entered delightedly
into a recital of the "mixup," and it turned
out that Mr. Tom and Mr. Burney were one.
It was like meeting an old friend; he seemed
as pleased as we and insisted on our going

up to his ranch; he said "the missus" would feel slighted if we passed her by. So we turned into another lane, and presently drew up before the ranch house. "The missus" came dancing out to meet us, and right welcome she made us feel. Mr. Burney went back to bring the rest, but they were already setting up the tents and had supper almost ready. However, we stayed and had supper with the Burneys.

They are powerfully happy and talked eagerly of themselves and their prospects. "It's just grand to have a home of your own and some one to do for. I just *love* to mend for Tommy, but I always hated to mend before," said the missus.

"You bet," Mr. Burney answered, "it is sure fine to know there's somebody at home with a pretty pink dress on, waitin' for a fellow when he comes in from a long day in the saddle."

And so they kept up their thoughtless chatter; but every word was as a stab to poor Aunt

# BUDDY AND BABY GIRL

Hettie. She had Baby Girl on her lap and was giving the children their supper, but I noticed that she ate nothing. It was easy to see that she was not strong. Baby Girl is four years old and is the fattest little thing. She has very dark blue eyes with long, black lashes, and the shortest, most turned-up little nose. She is so plump and rosy that even the faded old blue denim dress could not hide her loveliness.

Mrs. O'Shaughnessy could not keep her eyes off the children. "What is the little girl's name?" she asked.

"Caroline Agnes Lucia Lavina Ida Eunice," was the astonishing reply.

Mrs. O'Shaughnessy gasped. "My *good-ness*," she exclaimed; "is that *all?*"

"Oh, no," Aunt Hettie went on placidly; "you see, her mother could n't call her all the names, so she just used the first letters. They spell Callie; so that is what she called her. But I don't like the name. I call her Baby Girl."

## LETTERS ON AN ELK HUNT

I asked her how she ever came to name her that way, and she said, "My sister wanted a girl, but there were six boys before this little one came. Each time she hoped it would be a girl, and accordingly selected a name for a girl. So there were six names saved up, and as there was n't much else to give her, my sister gave them *all* to the baby."

After supper the Burneys rode down to camp with us. We had the same camping ground that we had when we came up. The cabin across the creek, where we met Grandma Mortimer, is silent and deserted; the young couple have moved away with their baby.

Mrs. O'Shaughnessy kept talking about the fight, and Mr. Burney gave us the history of the children. "Their mother," he began, "has been dead about eighteen months. She really died with a broken heart. Baby Girl was only a few weeks old when the father went to Alaska, and I guess he 's dead. He was to 'a' been back in three years, and no one has ever heard a word from him. His name was

# BUDDY AND BABY GIRL

Bolton; he was a good fellow, only he went bughouse over the gold fields and just fretted till he got away — sold everything for a grub stake — left his wife and seven kids almost homeless. But they managed some way till the mother died. With her last breath she asked that the two youngest be kept together; she knew the oldest ones would have to be separated. She never did give up looking for Bolton and she wanted him to have the babies.

"Her sister Hettie has worked around here for years; her and Rob Langley have been going to marry ever since I can remember, but always there has something cropped up. And now that Hettie has got to take care of the kids I guess they won't never marry; she won't burden him with them. It is hard for her to support them, too. Work is scarce, and she can't get it, lots of times, because of the kids."

The Burneys soon went home and the rest of us went to bed, — all except Mrs. O'Shaughnessy, who was so cranky and snappy that we left her by the fire. It seemed hours after when I awoke. She was still sitting by the fire; she was absently marking in the ashes with a stick. I happened to be the first one up next morning and as I stirred up the fire I saw "Baby" written in the ashes. We had breakfasted and the men had gone their ways when Mrs. O'Shaughnessy said to me, —

"It is a blessed old soul Mrs. Mortimer is. Do you mind any good lesson that she taught us in the cabin beyont?" I did not remember. "She said, 'The pangs of motherhood make us mothers not only of our own, but of every child that needs mothering, — especially if our own little children need us no longer. Fill their little places with ones who do need us.' Them's her very words, and it's sweet truth it is. Both my Katie and Sheridan have been grown and gone these many years and my heart has ached for childher, and there's none but Cora Belle. I am goin' to get them childher this day. What do you think about it?"

## BUDDY AND BABY GIRL

I thought so well of it that in about two minutes we were harnessing the horses and were off to lay the plan before Hettie in record-breaking time.

Poor Hettie: she wept quietly while the advantages of the scheme were being pointed out. She said, " I love the children, dearly, but I am not sure I can always feed and clothe them; that has worried me a lot. I am almost sure Bolton is dead. I 'll miss the little things, but I am glad to know they are well provided for. You can take them."

" Now," said Mrs. O'Shaughnessy, " you go on an' marry your man if he is a decent sort. Do it right away before something else happens. It is an illigant wedding present I 'll be sendin' you. You must come to see the childher often. What 's the b'y's name ? "

" We never did name him; you see we had kind of run out of boys' names. We just called him Buddy."

" I can find a name for him," said Mrs. O'Shaughnessy. " Is there a Joseph in the family?" Hettie said no. "Well, then, he is named Joseph Bolton O'Shaughnessy, and I'll have them both baptized as soon as we get to Green River."

So in the morning we start with two new members. Mrs. O'Shaughnessy is very happy. I am so glad myself that I can hardly express myself. We are *all* happy except Mr. Murry; he has at last given up hopes, and gone. Mr. Haynes growls a little about having to travel along with a rolling nursery, but he is just bluffing. I am longing to see Junior. We have not heard one word since we left them, and I am so homesick for mother and my boy. And *you*, best of friends, when shall I see your beloved face? To-morrow night we shall camp at Ten Trees and we shall be one day nearer home.

With much love,<br>
ELINORE RUPERT STEWART.

# XII

## A STAMPEDE

My dear, dear Friend, —

It is with a chastened, humble heart that I begin this letter; I have stood face to face with tragedy and romance, and to me one is as touching as the other, but you will know better when I tell you what I mean. We *all* bustled about to get started from Newfork. Now that we had started, all were homesick. Just ahead of us was a drove of two thousand steers being driven to the railroad to be shipped. I advise you to keep ahead of such drives when you take such a trip, because the trampling of so many feet makes a road almost impassable. What had been snow in the mountains had been rain on the desert, and we found the going decidedly bad. A

143

rise of a hill would give us, now and then, a glimpse of a slow-moving, dark-colored mass of heaving forms, and the desert breezes brought to our ears the mournful lowing of the poor creatures. Sometimes, too, we could hear a snatch of the cowboys' songs. It was all very beautiful and I would have enjoyed it hugely except that my desire to be home far outran the wagon and I felt like a prisoner with clogs.

We nooned at the cabin of Timothy Hobbs, but no one was at home; he at last had gone "back East" for Jennie. About mid-afternoon the boss of the cow outfit came up on a splendid horse. He was a pleasant fellow and he made a handsome picture, with his big hat, his great chaps and his jangling spurs, as he rode along beside our wagons, talking.

He told us that a crazy duffer had gone about over the desert for years digging wells, but at last he struck water. A few miles ahead was a well flowing like an artesian well. There would be plenty of water for

144

every one, even the cattle. Next morning we could start ahead of the herds and so the roads would be a little better.

It was quite early when we made camp in the same long draw where we saw Olaf. There was a great change. Where had been dry, burning sand was now a clear little stream that formed shallow pools where the sand had blown away, so that harder soil could form a bottom less greedy than the sand. Off to our left the uneasy herd was being held in a wide, flat valley. They were grazing on the dry, sparse herbage of the desert. Quite near the well the mess-wagon had stopped and the cook was already preparing supper. Beyond, a few yards away, a freighter's long outfit was stopped in the road.

Did you ever see the kind of freight outfit that is used to bring the great loads across the desert? Then I 'll tell you about the one we camped near. Freight wagons are not made precisely like others; they are very much larger and stronger. Several of these are coupled together; then as many teams as is necessary are hitched on — making a long, unbroken string of wagons. The horses are arranged in the same manner as the wagons. Great chains are used to pull the wagons, and when a camp is made the whole affair is stopped in the middle of the road and the harness is dropped right where the horse that bore it stood. Many freighters have what they call a coaster hitched to the last wagon. The coaster is almost like other wagons, but it is a home on wheels; it is built and furnished as sheep wagons are. This freighter had one, and as we drove past I was surprised to see the form of a woman and a small boy. We camped quite near them.

For an hour we were very busy preparing supper and arranging for the night. As we sat at supper I thought I had never known so quiet and peaceful an hour. The sun hung like a great, red ball in the hazy west. Purple

146

shadows were already gathering. A gentle wind rippled past across the dun sands and through the gray-green sage.

The chain parts of the hobbles and halters made a clinking sound as the horses fed about. Presently we heard a rumbling just like distant thunder. The cowboys sprang into their saddles; we heard a shot, and then we knew the terrible truth, — the steers had stampeded. For me, the next few minutes were an eternity of frightful confusion. Mrs. O'Shaughnessy and I found ourselves with the children upon our largest wagon; that was absolutely all the protection to be had. It would have gone down like a house of cards if that heaving sea of destruction had turned our way. I was scared witless. Mrs. O'Shaughnessy knelt among the children praying with white lips. I stood up watching the terrible scene. The men hastily set the horses free. There was no time to mount them and ride to safety with so many little children, and as there was nothing to tie them to but the wagons; we *had* to let them go so as to have the wagons left for shelter. *This* is why cowboys are such well-loved figures of romance and in mentioning them romance is fact.

"Greater love hath *no* man than this : that he lay down his life for his brother." They knew nothing about us only that we were defenseless. They rode boldly on their stanch little horses flanking the frenzied steers, shooting a leader here and there as they got a chance. If an animal stumbled it went down to its death, for hundreds of pounding hoofs would trample it to pulp. So it would have been with the boys if their horses had stepped into a badger hole or anything of the kind had happened. So the tide was turned, or the steers kept of themselves, I don't know which, on up the valley instead of coming up our draw. The danger was past.

Presently the cowboys came straggling back. Mrs. O'Shaughnessy ran to meet them. So when two on one horse came with a third riding close beside, helping to hold an injured man on, we knew some one was hurt. Mrs. O'Shaughnessy was, as usual, ready and able to help.

But the freighter's daughter was as quick and had a mattress ready beside the coaster by the time the cowboys came up with the wounded man. Gently the men helped their comrade to the mattress and gently Mrs. O'Shaughnessy and the girl began their work. I quieted the children and put them to bed. The men were busy rounding up the horses. The cowboys kept talking together in low tones and coming and going in twos and threes. They acted so queerly that I wondered if some one else was not hurt. I asked the boss if any more of his men were hurt. He said no, none of *his* men were. I knew none of our men or the freighter were harmed, so I dismissed fear and went to Mrs. O'Shaughnessy.

"Poor boy," she said, "he has a broken thigh and he's hurt inside. His belly is knocked into a cocked-hat. We will pull him through. A man has already gone back to Newfork to get an automobile. They will take him to Rock Springs to the hospital in the morning."

Mrs. O'Shaughnessy and the girl were doing all that could be done; they sent me back to care for the children. To keep warm I crawled under the blankets, but not to sleep. It did n't seem to me that I could *ever* sleep again. I could hear the men talking in subdued tones. The boss was dispatching men to different places. Presently I saw some men take a lantern and move off toward the valley. I could see the light twinkling in and out among the sage-brush. They stopped. I could see forms pass before the light. I wondered what could be the matter. The horses were all safe; even Boy, Mr. Haynes's dog, was safe, shivering and whining on his master's blankets. I could plainly hear the hiccoughs of the wounded man: the click-cluck, click-cluck, kept on with maddening

150

persistence, but at last his nurses forced enough hot water down him to cause vomiting. The blood-clots came and the poor fellow fell asleep. A lantern was hung upon the wagon and the two women went into the coaster to make some coffee.

It was three o'clock in the morning when the men of our outfit came back. They put on their heavy coats and were seeing to their horses. I asked Clyde what was the matter.

"Hush," he said; "lie still. It is Olaf."

"But I want to help," I said.

"You can't help. It's — all over," he replied as he started again to where the lantern was gleaming like a star fallen among the sage.

I tucked the children in a little more snugly, then went over to the coaster.

"Won't you come to bed and rest?" I asked Mrs. O'Shaughnessy.

"No, I'll not. Are me children covered and warm?"

"Yes," I answered.

"What are them fellys pow-wowing about down in the sage?"

"Olaf is dead," I said.

"Who says God is not merciful? Now all the poor felly's troubles are done with. 'Twas him that caused the stampede, mayhap. God send him peace. I am glad. He will never be hungry nor cold any more."

"Yes," said the girl; speaking slowly. "I am glad, too. He almost lived in this draw. We saw him every trip and he *did* suffer. Dad left a little for him to eat and whatever he could to wear every trip. The sheep-herders helped him, too. But he suffered. All the home he had was an old, thrown-away sheep wagon down beyond the last ridge toward the valley. I've seen him every two weeks for ten years. It's a wonder he has not been killed before."

"I wonder," said Mrs. O'Shaughnessy, "if he has any family. Where will they bury him?"

"He has no people. If they will listen to

# A STAMPEDE

Dad, they will lay him here on the desert. He would want it so."

After breakfast Mrs. O'Shaughnessy lay down for a little rest. When the wounded man awoke the girl gave him a little coffee.

"You're awful good to me," he said. "I'd like to have you around all the time."

The girl smiled gravely. "Ain't you got nobody to take care of you?"

"No. What is your name?"

"Amy Winters. Now you must hush. Talkin' might make you worse."

"I'm not so tur'ble bad off. Where do you live?"

"In the coaster, somewhere on the road between Pinedale and Rock Springs. Dad is a freighter."

"Huh! Do you like to live that way?"

"No; I want a house and a garden awful bad, but Dad can't do nothin' but freight and we've got Jessie to raise. We ain't got no ma."

"Do women *have* to change their names when they marry?"

153

"I don't know. Reckon they do, though. Why?"

"'Cause my name is Tod Winters. I know where there is a dandy little place up on the Gros Ventre where a cabin would look mighty good to me if there was some one to keep it for me — "

"Oh, say," she interrupted, "that is a awful pretty handkerchief you've got around your neck."

Just then the automobile came up frightening our horses. I heard no more, but the "awful pretty handkerchief" was missing when the hero left for the hospital. They used some lumber from a load the freighter had and walled up a grave for Olaf. They had no tools but axes and a shovel we had along. By noon Olaf was buried. Glenholdt set a slab of sandstone at the head. With his knife he had dug out these words — "Olaf. The friend of horses."

We camped last night at Ten Trees. To-night we are at Eden Valley. The mystery

## A STAMPEDE

of Mrs. O'Shaughnessy's sudden change about the license is explained. She unloaded an elk at the Sanders cabin. "'T was two I aimed to bring you, but me own family has increased by twins whilst I've been gone, so one ilk will have to do you."

So now, dear friend, I am a little nearer you. In one more week I shall be home.

Sincerely, *thankfully* yours,

E. A. S.

# XIII

NEARING HOME

DEAR FRIEND, —

We shall reach Green River City to-night. We will rest the teams one day, then start home. It will take us two days from Green River to reach home, so this is the last letter on the road. When we made camp here last night we saw some one coming on horseback along the cañon rim 'on the opposite side. The form seemed familiar and the horse looked like one I had seen, but I dared not believe my eyes. Clyde, who was helping to draw water from the eighty-foot well without a pulley, thought I was bereft as I ran from the camp toward the advancing rider. But although I thought what I saw must be a mirage, still I knew Mrs. Louderer on Bismarck.

156

# NEARING HOME

Out of breath from my run, I grasped her fat ankle and panted till I could speak.

"Haf they run you out of camp, you iss so bad?" she asked me by way of greeting. Then, more kindly, "Your boy iss all right, the mutter also. I am come, though, to find you. It iss time you are home with the *kinder*. Haf you any goose-grease left?"

I had, all she had given me.

At camp, joy knew no bounds. Never was one more welcome than our beloved neighbor. Her astonishment knew no bounds either, when her big blue eyes rested upon Mrs. O'Shaughnessy's "twins."

"Frau O'Shaughnessy," she said severely, "what have you here? You iss robbed an orphan asylum. How haf you come by these?"

Mrs. O'Shaughnessy is so full of life and good spirits and so delighted to talk about her "childher" that she gave a very animated recital of how she became a happy mother. In turn Mrs. Louderer told how she grew more and more alarmed by our long absence, but decided not to alarm the neighbors, so she had "made a search party out of mineself," and had fared forth to learn our fate.

We had a merry supper; even Haynes became cheerful, and there was no lagging next morning when we started for home. When people go on elk hunts they are very likely to return in tatters, so I am going to leave it to your imagination to picture our appearance when we drove up to the rear of the hotel about sundown. Our friend Mrs. Hutton came running to meet us. I was ashamed to go into her house, but she leaned up against the house and laughed until tears came. "*What* chased you?" she gasped. "You must have been run through some of those barbed wire things that they are putting up to stop the German army."

Mrs. Hutton is a little lady who bolsters up self-respect and makes light of trying situations, so she "shooed" us in and I sneaked into my room and waited until Clyde

NEARING HOME

could run down to the store and purchase me
a dress. I feel quite clean and respectable
now, sitting up here in my room writing this
to you. I will soon be at home now. Until
then good-bye.

E. R. S.

## XIV

### THE MEMORY-BED

October 25.

DEAR, DEAR FRIEND, —

Can you guess how happy I am? Be it *ever* so humble there is no place like home.

It is so good to sit in my creaky old rocker, to hold Junior, to feel his dear weight; to look at my brave little mother. I do not like the "in-law." She is *mother* to me. Under the east window of our dining-room we have a flower-bed. We call it our memory-bed because Clyde's first wife had it made and kept pansies growing there. We poured the water of my little lost boy's last bath onto the memory-bed. I keep pansies growing in one side of the bed in memory of her who loved them. In the other end I plant sweet alyssum in memory of my baby. A few pansies and a tuft of sweet alyssum smiled a welcome,

160

# THE MEMORY-BED

though all the rest of my flowers were dead. We have a hop-vine at the window and it has protected the flowers in the memory-bed. How happy I have been, looking over the place! Some young calves have come while we were gone; a whole squirming nest full of little pigs. My chickens have outgrown my knowledge. There is no snow here at all. Our experiences on our trip seem almost unreal, but the wagonload of meat to be attended to is a reminder of realities. I have had a fine trip; I have experienced about all the human emotions. I had not expected to encounter so many people or to get the little inside glimpses that I 've had, but wherever there are human beings there are the little histories. I have come home realizing anew how happy I am, how much I have been spared, and how many of life's blessings are mine. Poor Mrs. Louderer, childless and alone, openly envying Mrs. O'Shaughnessy her babies! In my bedroom there is a row of four little brown heads asleep on their pil-

LETTERS ON AN ELK HUNT

lows. Four precious kiddies all my own.
And not the least of my blessings, *you* to tell
my happiness to. Has my trip interested
you, dear friend? I *hope* you liked it. It will
lose a little of its charm for me if you find it
uninteresting.

I will write you again soon.

Your happy friend,

E. R. S.


THE END

**COSIMO** is a specialty publisher of books and publications that inspire, inform, and engage readers. Our mission is to offer unique books to niche audiences around the world.

**COSIMO BOOKS** publishes books and publications for innovative authors, nonprofit organizations, and businesses. **COSIMO BOOKS** specializes in bringing books back into print, publishing new books quickly and effectively, and making these publications available to readers around the world.

**COSIMO CLASSICS** offers a collection of distinctive titles by the great authors and thinkers throughout the ages. At **COSIMO CLASSICS** timeless works find new life as affordable books, covering a variety of subjects including: Business, Economics, History, Personal Development, Philosophy, Religion & Spirituality, and much more!

**COSIMO REPORTS** publishes public reports that affect your world, from global trends to the economy, and from health to geopolitics.

FOR MORE INFORMATION CONTACT US AT
**INFO@COSIMOBOOKS.COM**

❊ if you are a book lover interested in our current catalog of books

❊ if you represent a bookstore, book club, or anyone else interested in special discounts for bulk purchases

❊ if you are an author who wants to get published

❊ if you represent an organization or business seeking to publish books and other publications for your members, donors, or customers.

**COSIMO BOOKS ARE ALWAYS
AVAILABLE AT ONLINE BOOKSTORES**

VISIT COSIMOBOOKS.COM
BE INSPIRED, BE INFORMED

CPSIA information can be obtained at www.ICGtesting.com
Printed in the USA
LVOW08s0238110813

347256LV00001B/243/A